deLIVEReD

Lisa's Story

Lisa and Reid Barker

ISBN-13: 9781522704201
ISBN-10: 1522704205

This book is dedicated to the greatest hero I never knew, my organ donor, Courtney, who saved my life.

PURPOSE

Our hope as you read this book is that you will see the amazing grace and love of our Lord, Jesus Christ. We share our story in order to bring more glory to His name for the amazing miracle He worked and is continuing to work in our lives. Our prayer is that the beauty of organ donation is made clearly evident to you and that you will consider becoming an organ donor. Also, our hope is that God will use our words to stir up a deeper, or even new, love and passion for Him in your life. He loves you, cares for you, and pursues you. God bless!

—Team Barker

CONTENTS

PROLOGUE: SEVEN MINUTES

My heart was racing. I could feel that lump in my throat more than ever—the one you read about but maybe only experience a few times in your life to this extreme. The orange-and-blue helicopter sitting there, being quickly prepped for takeoff, would soon carry the most prized cargo. That same CareFlite helicopter that often sparks spontaneous prayers on sight for strangers you know are in trouble would soon carry my beautiful wife and high-school sweetheart, Lisa, to Baylor Hospital in Dallas.

"OK, guys, this is as far as you go. We'll take good care of her." I could barely hear the words from the CareFlite nurse as the propellers kicked on. "Do y'all want to watch them take off or leave now? They will be there fast...seven minutes."

"Budd–Chiari, dialysis, intubation, liver and kidney failure..." The doctor's words kept replaying in my mind. *How did we get here? We were supposed to be discharged and home hours ago. We are only twenty-five. It was a simple gallbladder removal!*

Lisa's mom and I needed to leave now! We couldn't find the car fast enough in that parking garage at Baylor Plano. "She will be there in seven minutes..." Time seemed to be flying by and standing still at the same time. *It has to have already been about four minutes. We've got to hurry. I don't want her being there alone.* My thoughts were jumbled and sporadic.

"She was so awake and alert! I want y'all to know how huge that is!" Those small words of encouragement from our dear friend and retired nurse, Peggy, to Lisa's mom, Cheryl, and me resonated through all the mental fog. I looked for any reassurance to cling to. The doctors and nurses had tried to give that comfort, but their faces that Tuesday in the ICU told a truth that their mouths could not hide.

The frankness of the doctor's words in the ICU waiting room earlier had pierced my core: "This is going to get much worse before it can get better." The truth of those words was simple. My high-school sweetheart was fading fast, and not even two years into marriage, we were in a fight for her life.

CHAPTER 1

THE BEGINNING OF TEAM BARKER

Lisa

"**H**ave you met the new baseball player?"

This was a common question I heard throughout the first week of my junior year of high school. I remember seeing Reid, the new baseball player, for the first time in our school cafeteria. After meeting him, I remember thinking how cute he was but also how nice and respectful he was. Those traits did not go hand in hand for many high-school boys.

Our second semester of our junior year was when we really got to know each other because we had two classes together. Reid transferred into my math class, and when I saw him, I had to move seats to be closer to him. My crush on Reid started then. If you'd ever told me I would find my husband in high school, I would have laughed and thought you were crazy. God obviously had a different plan, and little did I know that our future together would begin that day. We dated through college and began careers, and then Reid asked me the most anticipated question of my life: "Will you marry me?"

Reid

July 6, 2012, was by far the happiest day of our lives—our wedding day! This was a day many of us had been anxiously awaiting for a long time. We had our friends and family surrounding us that whole weekend, and one of our best friends, Blake Simpson, was marrying us.

Lisa and I had been dating for seven years. We shared many of the same friends, and our long relationship had given our families a close bond that we really enjoyed. In high school she was a gorgeous blond cheerleader whom I had fallen for.

I had transferred from a private high school in Garland, Texas, to a 5A public school, Naaman Forest, down the road. It was a move that I welcomed with nervousness and excitement. I was especially looking forward to playing high-school baseball with a handful of guys I had grown up playing select ball with. Lisa and I still look back at all the times she would come to watch my team, made up of our mutual friends, play when we were twelve years old. Little did she know that the kid in center field whom she had never met would one day be her husband. It is crazy how God works.

Lisa

Our faith has always been a part of our relationship. We both were very blessed and grew up with parents who loved the Lord and led us to have a personal relationship with Jesus Christ. Reid and I started attending church together in high school and attended off and on throughout college. When we got engaged, we took a premarital course called "Before You Say I Do." Once we married, we thoroughly enjoyed being encouraged, growing in our faith, and learning with other married couples.

Reid

Lisa's favorite thing to do at weddings is to watch the groom's reaction when he catches a glimpse of the bride for the first time.

Our wedding photographer was able to capture that moment, as I glanced at my dad, Rick, who was also my best man. Tears filled my eyes, and a huge smile came across my face as I saw Lisa for the first time that day. Seeing my bride at the end of that aisle is a memory I will never forget. That moment truly exemplified our journey so far. My buddies Cody Gambill and Travis Latz had the honor of opening the doors to reveal my bride in her beautiful dress. Seeing her when those doors opened and her long walk down the aisle reminded me of meeting her and all the memories we had made along the way. As she walked, she passed the mesmerized faces of our wedding guests. These were the people we shared many of our joyous memories with and would desperately lean on in the years to come.

Lisa and I spoke often about how it was apparent God had created each of us with the other in mind. She was like no girl I had ever met. The way she loved people and life was rare for a popular, beautiful young girl. I will openly admit, using the coaching term, I definitely out punted my coverage. God hooked it up!

For our ceremony we decided to write our own vows, and I meant these words with all my heart when I said them to her that day: "Lisa, I will be by your side throughout every blessing, every trial, and all situations in between that life may bring us. In good health and in bad, I will cherish the time God has given me with you and promise to take care of you in all times of need." Little did we know, not even two years into marriage, how intensely those vows would be challenged.

Lisa

Reid and I both love people and investing in relationships. We try to keep in contact with old and new friends with dinner dates, e-mails, texts, and phone calls. Relationships are so important to us, and our family and friends are so special to us.

In July of 2013, Reid and I got to travel to Ghana, West Africa, along with some of our dearest friends for a two-week mission trip. This was my fifth trip to Ghana and Reid's first. I was beyond excited for him to experience Ghana and to meet so many of my Ghanaian friends whom I had grown very close to throughout the years. We did a medical mission the first week, and the second week we were in the village of Mamakrom with the ESI (Every Soul's Important) Foundation, which our friends Linda and Rusty Simpson founded in 2006.

The village of Mamakrom is so dear to our hearts. We sponsor two sweet children there and have loved watching them grow and seeing all that God has done through this village. God laid on my heart during my 2011 trip to Ghana how important it was that Reid and I experience Ghana together in 2013. I now see why that was so important.

Reid

Three words: Excellence Playa Mujeres. This resort outside of Cancun is where Lisa and I spent our honeymoon, and we anticipated a holiday trip back with our friends Drake and Jenna Thornton to bring a fresh start to a new year in 2014. Before this trip Lisa and I had been trying to eat really healthily and had seen some good results. We both worked out regularly and were in seemingly great health.

So off we went for another dream vacation in our honeymoon spot. Life was perfect. We were enjoying this nice break from our careers. Lisa was in her third year as a dental hygienist, and I was on Christmas break from teaching and coaching in Frisco, Texas.

While we were napping on the beach in the Caribbean one afternoon, a Facebook message came through my phone from Lisa's brother, Brian. I could not wrap my mind around his words. One of our coaches at Pioneer Heritage Middle School, where I worked, had suffered a massive stroke and passed away. He was thirty-nine. Shock, sorrow, and disbelief were rushing through my mind. It was a quick shake back to the reality of life. Coach Furnas and I had grown pretty close over the last few years, and I selfishly wondered how school would be without him. As we sat on our beach chairs, Lisa leaned over and did the only thing we knew to do in these situations: she prayed for the peace and comfort for Furnas's family that can only be found in Christ.

I remember the conversation Lisa and I had that night in Mexico about how crazy it is that we never really know what is going on inside our bodies. Oh, the irony in that moment. We did not know what was going on in her body, a somatic battlefield that was being prepared for us in our near future back in the States. Happy New Year! Welcome to 2014!

2005 | First photo together

Wedding 7/6/2012
Photo taken by Leslie Spurlock

Ghana Mission Trip 2013 | Betty and Nathaniel
Our sponsor children in Mamakrom

CHAPTER 2

ONE IN A MILLION

Lisa

The weekend of January 31, 2014, was an exciting time. We were celebrating bachelor and bachelorette activities for our dear friends Jessica and Blake, who had married us. The plan was that Friday night the guys and girls would enjoy separate activities and then would come together for a combination party Saturday night.

After Friday night's events, I started to not feel well. It was a hard decision for me, but I decided not to go to the celebratory bachelorette events on Saturday, February 1. I was not feeling well all day. I started to develop strong stomach pains, was sick to my stomach, and would take one bite of food and feel full. My upper abdomen was swollen and felt hot. I called my mother to tell her about my symptoms, and she urged me to go to the hospital that night, but I decided to wait until Sunday when Reid got home to see if the pain was still there.

By nature Reid and I are the type of people who assume that the pain is less serious and more in our heads than anything. We never want to be the ones making something out of nothing.

Reid got home in the early morning on Sunday. That morning my symptoms were still present, so we headed to my family doctor, who has weekend hours.

Waiting outside in the blistering cold on February 2, until the office opened, I had every possible scenario running through my mind. My family doctor was not on call that day. The doctor I saw listened to the symptoms I described, and when she took a look at my swollen abdomen and felt how hot it was, she referred me to Baylor Plano ER right away, because she did not have the necessary people at the office to run the tests I needed. She called the ER to tell them I was coming. She requested I be tested for pancreatitis.

We got in the car to drive to Baylor Plano, and I started crying and immediately Googled "pancreatitis." I knew this was quickly becoming more serious than I thought. Reid assured me like he always does that everything was going to be fine and told me to stay calm. He is always my sounding board.

Reid

Every possible minor WebMD diagnosis was racing through my mind. As a husband it is hard to describe the feeling you get when your wife is having health issues. All I could do was pray that the Lord would cover us and make her feel better. If I could have, I would have traded places with her then. Anything to take her pain and fear away. I refused to let my mind believe that her diagnosis could be something serious.

Lisa

We were taken back to the ER quickly, and after a sonogram was performed and blood was taken, a physician assistant came into the room to tell me that the sonogram revealed that my gallbladder was thickened and would most likely need to come out.

When the general surgeon came in, she informed us that, yes, my gallbladder did need to be removed, but she also mentioned the first words about my liver. She told us that my liver and spleen were enlarged and that she would do a liver biopsy while in surgery to see what was causing this swelling. I remember thinking how sweet and compassionate this surgeon was. She was about eight months pregnant and was radiating with joy. Little did we know she would be an angel for us over the next few days.

They admitted me into the hospital that night and told me I would have gallbladder-removal surgery on Monday morning. I was not able to eat anything and had not had much to eat all day. I was quickly becoming extremely thirsty. It was Super Bowl Sunday, and we were supposed to be at a church watch party. I remember lying in my hospital bed and watching the halftime show. My mom and mother-in-law left Reid and me to get some sleep. I remember seeing the emotion on my mother's face. She hated seeing her baby hurting, and it was also the first time I had been seriously ill as a married woman, which meant Reid was now taking care of her baby girl. I could not imagine what she was going through as a mother.

We had a restless night of sleep, and the nursing staff did their best to keep me comfortable throughout the night. Since my surgery was added late Sunday night, my surgery time was not until around ten o'clock Monday morning, February 3. My mom, Cheryl, joined us that morning, and she and Reid were with me as they wheeled me into surgery. Mom and Reid took a happy picture together, and Reid and I took one, too, right before they wheeled me in. We were happy and hopeful that this gallbladder removal would make me feel much better. I do not believe any of us were really concerned about the liver and spleen being enlarged at that time. I was not even sure what that meant.

My memory after that point becomes a little blurry. I remember waking up from surgery in my room and feeling nauseous and weak. I remember them telling me I had four little incisions because the surgery was done laparoscopically. The surgeon took pictures during the surgery and drained a liter and a half of fluid from around my liver. She showed us the pictures and had informed Reid and my mom that the appearance of my liver was not ideal. My gallbladder surgeon ordered an MRI for that day.

The afternoon quickly turned into evening, and I remember finally being wheeled down for an MRI. At this point we were still trying to rule out a serious liver condition. I had a very rough time with the MRI because I was so sick. We got the MRI done in an hour, and I remember being wheeled back up to my hospital room. My memory of Monday night and Tuesday is very spacey. I do not recall much of that time even though I had friends who came to visit and took pictures with me. Reid told me I was texting friends and family updates of my condition, but I have no memory of this.

Reid

One of the first possibilities discussed about Lisa's liver was that the swelling was caused by a hemangioma. This was a benign tumor that we were told would most likely not even need to be removed if the test results confirmed that diagnosis. I knew Lisa would be staying the night at the hospital, so I ran out to my school to get my sub plans ready and then home to pack a small bag. I was relieved that something more serious had not been found. Before walking out the door to head back to the hospital, I stopped in the kitchen to grab a bottled water. On our refrigerator Lisa and I have a dry-erase board. During our first two years of marriage, we'd used it to write reminders and, more often, encouraging notes to each other. I wrote in large letters, "Welcome home, Mrs. Barker." She got excited about little things like that, so I knew she would love walking in to see that note the next day, when she was discharged from the hospital.

I arrived back at Lisa's hospital room, and she was still getting her MRI. When they wheeled her in, I could see she was not doing well at all. She said it was horrible. With all the pain and nausea meds she had been on, she had seemed pretty out of it all day. I could not really have a conversation with her; I would just get quick one to two-word answers. She was going in and out of sleep every couple of minutes.

After Cheryl left, I prepped my fold-out chair for my night's sleep. I remember praying over and over that the MRI test results would come back quickly and be clear. How awesome would that be—a scan done after a surgeon had physically seen the exterior of her liver, knowing something was off, revealing nothing internally. Our God has worked bigger miracles. About that time the door opened. It was Lisa's night nurse. She looked first at Lisa, who was asleep, and then her gaze caught mine.

"Your surgeon just called and has ordered a CT scan first thing tomorrow morning."

My heart dropped. As soon as she left, tears began to fill my eyes. Something was not right. This was not good. If it was nothing, if everything was fine, she would not need another test. I put my hand on Lisa's leg and said another prayer, crying out for protection. I fell into a short, light sleep that night with a heavy heart and a worrying mind.

Monday morning was probably one of the toughest days of my life. I sat helpless, minute by minute, as I watched new people come into Lisa's hospital room to run tests, offer medicine that never seemed to help, and poke her with more needles. I was still reaching for anything that would give hope and continuing relentlessly to deny that something more serious was taking place. I truly felt if my faith was big enough, nothing bad would happen to Lisa, but my faith needed to be focused on the truth: if something bad was happening, it was God's plan.

Around ten thirty Lisa's gallbladder surgeon came into the room. Lisa was awake, but I could tell she was under heavy doses of pain medication. The doctor had a loving, compassionate, yet fearful look in her eyes. She was young, but she had a great bedside manner and a calmness that you would typically expect only from someone much older and further in her career. She told us that they would not be conducting a CT scan and that she had spent all night awake studying Lisa's MRI, which had diagnosed Lisa with a liver condition known as Budd–Chiari.

She further explained, "You see, her liver is in bad shape."

Obviously, I had never heard of this condition. My next question to the doctor was, "Is this condition common?"

Her answer caught me completely off guard. "This condition is incredibly rare. It only affects one in a *million* people!"

To give you some perspective, that is like being the only person living in Austin, Texas, or San Jose, California, with this condition.

That relentless spirit I'd had only moments earlier of fighting the unknown reality of the situation instantly left me. The weight of her statement fell directly on my heart. Any feeling I'd previously had of helplessness magnified times ten. *How do you even go about beating something that only one in a million people deal with? Is there even research or a cure for something that rare?* These were just the beginning doubts and questions in my mind.

The doctor proceeded to tell us that Lisa would have to be moved to Baylor Dallas Hospital in order to see their liver specialist. At this point everything still seemed to be relatively OK in the grand scheme of things. We would probably even be driving Lisa to Dallas by ourselves. Oh, how quickly things can change.

Unbeknown to us, Lisa was doing much worse than we thought. A change in plans meant she was now being moved to the ICU floor at Plano until she could be transported to Dallas. I saw Lisa's doctor in the hallway and pulled out one of the Ghana bracelets we had gotten from our mission trip to Africa. I had grabbed a couple of them from my cabinet at school to give to people at the hospital who were very kind to us. "I want to give this to you. It is a bracelet from our mission trip, and I know Lisa would want you to wear it and think about her and pray for her." The tears immediately welled up in my eyes, and she said she would always keep it. From there, we were headed to the ICU floor.

As my whole world was being completely shaken, I remember thinking, *Lord, what is going on? We are so young.* Everything in the last eighteen hours had happened so fast that it was hard to process. I began to get frustrated because I felt as if the nurses and doctors were not telling me everything. I know it was probably for my protection and in my best interest, but I wanted the honest truth. Was Lisa going to die? *Stop being vague, and cut to the chase. I don't want this to be a sudden surprise.*

I walked over to the window in that ICU room to try to distract myself for a moment. It made me more upset that everything looked "normal" outside those hospital walls. *That is the world we are supposed to be living in.* Tears began to well in my eyes again. Off in the distance, as I scanned the horizon, something caught my attention. It was the huge steeple of our church standing high above all the other trees and buildings in the surrounding area. Above every other thing in my view at that moment was the magnificent cross. "Wow, babe, you won't believe it. I can see our church steeple right here from your window."

God hears us and speaks to us. I know this because this is one of the many times that week He would listen and communicate with me. It is not always the way we anticipate; sometimes we just have to open our eyes and see His presence. God knew that I needed His loving reassurance in that moment. No matter how ferocious the storm and world around me was getting, God's promise was planted right there for me to see. He was lovingly showing me that His perspective is high above all others. Even when we do not feel like He is near, He is firmly planted there, right in the center of our storm, right where we need Him the most. Sometimes all we have to do is look.

The ICU door opened again, and this time a male doctor came into Lisa's room. He was debriefing us on their attempts to get Lisa into a bed at Baylor Dallas but said they still did not have an open ICU bed. He had an uneasy sense of urgency, and the idea of Lisa being driven to Dallas by us or ambulance, which originally seemed like the plan, faded very quickly. He said he was about to make a call in order to get her in there ASAP. This was another subtle way of expressing the increasing severity of her situation.

Finally, I could not take it anymore and asked him a very loaded question: "What should we expect when we get there?"

I was not sure I really wanted to know the answer to this question. It was one of those moments when you halfway plug your ears, knowing some loud noise or explosion is about to take place. Still, I could not bear being blindsided by tragedy.

"You can expect her to be in pretty critical condition. Her organs are really struggling right now, and the problem is, when one system shuts down, it causes something like a domino effect. Her kidneys appear to be shutting down, and there is a possibility she will be put on dialysis." He excused himself and went to make that call.

My eyes had kept glancing at Lisa while he had explained all of this, and, thankfully, she was falling in and out of a drug-induced, body-war sleep that would protect her from truly knowing or understanding what was going on. I was grateful she was not all that aware of what was happening to her. That would have added a whole different level of challenges in trying to encourage and comfort her during those crucial minutes.

"Mr. Barker, we are going to need you two to step out into the waiting room. They have a bed available in Dallas, and the CareFlite team will be here shortly to get her ready for flight."

How can I leave now? I need to stay here with her. I want to be by her side. I felt helpless.

Cheryl and I stepped into the waiting room, and it was as if we crossed an emotional barrier together. The dam broke that had been holding in our tears for fear of Lisa knowing, and we let the tears flow. Family and friends were waiting in that ICU waiting room, and I hugged a few and went into the bathroom. After I locked the door, I slid to the floor, leaned up against the wall, and sobbed. "Please, God…please do not take her." Understandable but selfish prayers began to pour from my heart. I was not "deal making" with God or promising to live better if He did this, but I was emphatically begging Him to perform a miracle. *I do not know a better person who loves people like she does. Why can't this be happening to me instead? She is too kind and gentle to be going through such pain. She is my teammate and best friend, the first person I see in the morning, and the one who has been by my side through everything the past eight years.* "Please, God…"

After I somewhat pulled myself together and emerged from the restroom, our families and close friends circled around, and we prayed. It is such a beautiful thing to have friends who will stand with you and be willing to go before the Creator of the universe with you in prayer.

Shortly after we finished praying, Lisa's gallbladder surgeon came out of the ICU doors. "They are about to take her down. You can either leave now if you want to be there waiting when she gets to Dallas, or you can ride down the elevator with her and watch her take off."

I wanted to see her again before she left. We had not had a chance to really tell her good-bye, and I did not know if I would ever talk to my wife again.

"They will take good care of her. I have to tell you, though, this is going to get much worse before it can get better."

Oh, the power of those words. Little did I know the weight and deep truth they would hold. They played over and over again in my mind: "This is going to get much worse before it can get better."

CHAPTER 3

ARRIVAL IN DALLAS

Reid

Cheryl and I jumped out of the car in front of Baylor Dallas Hospital, and Peggy went to park in the garage. Lisa's sister, Laura, had called to tell us she was on the fourth floor. I do not even know that Cheryl and I spoke on that elevator. What could be said? We were both trying to wake up from this nightmare. Ding! The elevator doors opened on the fourth floor, where we were greeted by Laura and Lisa's dad, Steve. "Reid, she wants you! She is asking for her husband."

I was so excited and relieved to know that Lisa was conscious. We had left Plano not knowing if we were ever going to be able to talk to her again, so the news of her personally requesting to see me was amazing. I turned the corner and walked down the long hallway toward her ICU room.

I remember passing friends of ours along the way, but I could not tell you who was there. It was one of the many out-of-body moments I would have during the next few days. Their faces were all a blur, and I was focused on what I would say to Lisa and trying to prepare myself for what I was about to see.

I came up to a set of double doors. I had a flashback to our wedding day. I got that similar nervousness I had had when waiting for the doors to open and seeing my bride for the first time, except these were not the tall double doors of a chapel. These double doors had an entirely different world behind them. These doors were not going to reveal the faces of our closest friends and family, and my bride in a white dress. No, these doors opened to a world of sickness, hurt, and strangers. Strangers I would instantly rely on to protect and save the most important person in my life.

The doors began to open, and Laura directed me to another room inside on the left. It was a scene straight out of an episode of *Grey's Anatomy*. My eyes caught Lisa's, and she gave me a big smile. One of the doctors asked if I was her husband and told me I could stand beside her. I never took my eyes off Lisa, but I could sense the organized chaos around me.

I stepped past the CareFlite team and wove my way around the other three nurses on the right side of her bed. She was in a large room that, upon further examination, was not just for her. There appeared to be three other occupied beds in that room. I touched Lisa's shoulder and began rubbing my fingers across her forehead and hair. I wanted to hold her hand, but the doctors were busy working on both of them.

"They said I am going into liver and kidney failure. They are giving me medicine to make me stay awake."

The calmness in Lisa's voice confused me, but then I realized the medicine was causing these effects. I could not understand why she was not freaking out, but I thanked God that she wasn't. It made it much easier for me to encourage her and focus on telling her how much I loved her instead of having to try to calm her nerves.

I knew things were serious, but I was still trying to figure out how bad they were. Then I looked over at the doctor working with Lisa's right arm. She had a tiny, needlelike device and was methodically sticking it into Lisa's wrist every couple of seconds. She'd probably made about eight needle pricks already and seemed intent on making more. I asked what she was doing, and she told me she was trying to find Lisa's pulse. Her blood pressure had gotten so low that they could not find a consistent pulse. In Lisa's other hand, another nurse was using a needle to inject some kind of drug to counteract the bad reaction Lisa had had to dopamine. Lisa's hand was puffy and cold and now covered in bloodied spots that resembled chicken pox.

"I love you so much, baby, and I am so proud of you. You are going to be OK. They are going to take care of you." I was trying, but I did not know what to say. All I wanted to do was crawl into that bed and hold her tight. I just wanted to switch places. *Let me take this on, God. Why does it have to be her? She doesn't deserve this. Please, give it to me.*

"Mrs. Lisa, we are going to give you some medicine to try to get your blood pressure up. If you start feeling light-headed or start getting a headache, let me know."

Only a few seconds after the medicine began to run through her veins, the ICU pod was filled with Lisa's screams. "*Ouch!* My chest—my chest hurts—it is hurting so bad!" Lisa screamed this over and over.

I saw the panic come over a new set of doctors' faces—the same look I had seen at Plano. "We are going to need y'all to step out," one said.

Sometime during this process, Cheryl had joined us in the room. They made us step into the little hallway outside and closed the door. We stood there and did the only thing we could. I hugged Cheryl as she said, "Oh, Reid."

After that, we didn't say a word. How do you verbalize the inevitable, and what comfort can you bring in that moment? We had always been close, but this would be our biggest trial faced together. I don't know how much time went by while we stood in that hall. As we waited, I walked into the main hall, which had grown more crowded with familiar faces. "Pray they can find a pulse," I insisted.

"Mr. Barker, we were able to get her stabilized, and you will be able to go in soon. Her body has been through so much in the past few hours, and we had to intubate her to allow her body to rest."

I was heartbroken. The words may as well have been knives being shoved into my eardrums. They hurt me to the core, and it was devastating news. I realized fully that Lisa was in very critical condition. *Surely it cannot get worse than this.* I did not have much knowledge of medically induced comas and intubation, but I had seen pictures and heard stories of loved ones making that gut-wrenching decision to take the most cherished person in their lives off the machines. *God, please do not let this end that way.*

Walking into that pod ICU room for the second time was completely different. It was much calmer now than it had been minutes ago. Tears began to form in my eyes as I saw my wife for the first time alive under the assistance of a machine. Her face no longer gave evidence of the internal war that was still being waged in her body. I looked nervously at the many tubes that were running out of her mouth, nose, and other ports that had been placed in her body. I watched as the ventilator rhythmically caused her chest to rise and fall. Her body temperature had dropped to ninety-four degrees, so they had placed an inflatable blanket that looked like a white swimming-pool float around her.

I could not grab her hand because it was buried somewhere underneath all the sheets and blankets, so I began to gently stroke her forehead. Her tongue was sticking out, wedged between her cheek and her breathing tube, but I dared not try to fix it. I was paranoid about bumping those tubes, even if they were held in place by things pasted to her cheeks. "I'm so sorry, baby. I love you so much. You are going to be OK. I know you are. Just please fight for us."

I didn't know if she could really hear me, but you hear crazy stories about patients hearing and responding while being in comas. For me, it was worth the effort, and it kept my mind occupied on staying positive for her.

This scene reminds me so much of our relationship with Christ. Sometimes we do not hear His voice, but He is always there, encouraging us and offering us that love and familiarity that we need. It is not until later that we see evidence of His faithfulness and know that He will always be there, even when we are not aware. I encourage you, in this moment, to recognize that the Creator of the universe is near to you. He does hear your cries, and He does care. Listen closely, and He will make His presence evident to you.

CHAPTER 4

STRAIGHT TO THE TOP

Reid

In the world of technology that we live in today, it did not take long for word to spread to everyone about Lisa's condition. People began showing up at the hospital to offer their support and to pray with us. I was even getting word from friends in Ghana who had heard the news and were praying nonstop around the clock for Lisa. You do not know faith until you experience the faith of our brothers and sisters in Ghana, West Africa. It is truly inspiring to witness them pouring out their hearts and advocating on the behalf of other believers. I can never express the gratitude I have for all of our friends who immediately started lifting us up in their prayers. They were heard and felt. That is truly the Body of Christ.

The hospital staff, seeing that the long hallway outside the ICU doors was becoming crowded with people, graciously offered us one of the consultation rooms. We now had some chairs and a place to store the immense amount of goodies that people were bringing to make our time there more comfortable.

For the most part, I did not want to be anywhere but by Lisa's side in the ICU room, but it was comforting to be surrounded by our close friends. It was somewhat comical how well known Lisa became for strangers on that hospital floor. Apparently, new arrivals seeking our location were quickly pointed in the direction of the "huge group down around the corner from the elevators."

That hallway would become a dwelling place for many of us over the next few days. It had such a unique sense of solitude and calm, while at the same time it was an avenue traveled by people who were in the most chaotic and frantic moments of their lives. I think people close to us knew they could not stay away. Lisa was important to so many people. She poured her heart and soul into making other people feel special, and one look down that hallway reflected all the hearts she had impacted. It was crazy to think she had no idea any of this was going on.

There were so many unanswered medical questions. I felt like the professionals were leaving me out of the loop of Lisa's situation. I know this was not really the case, but I could not help feeling so helpless. I cannot imagine what was going on behind the scenes and being said behind closed doors and what circumstances were being worked out by the medical staff. I know there were many unanswered questions for them as well.

I need to take this opportunity to offer my extreme gratitude for the amazing care Lisa got throughout her entire situation. Not one time were we made to feel like we were in the way, asking too many questions, or being bothersome. I have the utmost respect and appreciation for her entire medical team that aided in her care and for all medical professionals around the world. She had the most attentive, caring, and friendly nursing staff. It is hard to even find words to describe how caring each person was. Just another answered prayer. I am so thankful for our medical team and the countless hours of work that they do that often goes unseen. They are all living out Christ's love for people who need their help. I will be forever grateful.

Sometime late in the afternoon, the liver specialist came into the hallway and asked for me. It was difficult to be the point of communication in such serious discussions when I was only twenty-five years old. I was nervous that I was going to be asked to make decisions on Lisa's behalf that could alter the course of her life in a serious way. There is no premarital counseling that can prepare you to step into that role. These were bridges I thought we would have to cross eventually, but not until we had more wrinkles and gray hair. I prayed for clarity and strength from God to get me through all those situations that I would face in the days to come.

The liver specialist confirmed that Lisa did have Budd–Chiari, which caused severe blood clotting in her liver. He explained as best he could, to my limited understanding of medical jargon, that it was due to a genetic mutation in her blood, one that just happened somehow. Her bone marrow no longer shut off producing platelets, and this caused her blood to become extremely thick, resulting in the blood clots. It would be like pumping gas into your car and the handle getting stuck. Eventually, the gas is going to fill up in your tank and continue to flow out until it causes major issues or other damage.

The specialist then hit us with the news that would alter our lives forever. Her only chance of survival would be to get on the transplant list. Her liver, in the shape it was in, would not be able to keep her alive for long.

This was a terrifying thought. I did not know much about transplantation. It seemed like everything I had heard was that people were on the list for long periods of time, and it did not seem like Lisa was going to have much time. Even then, I had no idea what the success rates were for these types of surgeries.

He then went on to explain that they would have to do a bone-marrow biopsy the next morning in order to determine if a transplant was even possible with the type of blood disease she had. If her blood disease would not allow her body to accept and use a transplanted organ successfully, then they would not be able to perform one. With so many patients on the list, they could not risk losing a good organ in a hopeless situation. Barring any extreme change in plans, the doctor said the transplant-board committee would meet the next day around one o'clock in order to review Lisa's case and to either approve or reject her for the transplant list.

It seemed like the odds were stacked against her. It did not seem fair. What else could go wrong? I hated asking those things, because that question was soon answered.

"Lisa's kidneys are shutting down. We are going to have to hook her up to a dialysis machine. It will run continuously because her other organs are shutting down like her liver. It is like a chain reaction."

Just a couple of hours after I'd survived a round of jabs and right hooks to the face in the form of the blood-disease and transplant-list information, this news from the ICU doctor hit me like an uppercut right in the gut. I felt sick to my stomach. I got those pains in my throat and the back of my neck that you get when trying to fight back tears. This news shook all our friends and family in the waiting room. Her body was like a giant Jenga puzzle slowly being picked apart. Every couple of hours seemed to bring some foundation-shaking change in the course of her future. Would she be able to hold on through tomorrow?

Knowing that I was going to be staying at the hospital for an uncertain period of time, I agreed to go with my parents to our apartment to pack another bag. The car ride home was about twenty minutes, and it was mostly silent except for our tears. I had been holding it together fairly well at the hospital, but the tears flowed more freely around my parents. The levee broke as I entered our apartment. Flipping on the kitchen light so I could see where I was going, I caught a glance of the note I had left Lisa on the refrigerator: "Welcome home, Mrs. Barker!"

Oh, how our world had flipped upside down since I had written that note only the day before! Now there was a huge possibility that Lisa would never walk into our apartment again. My mind began racing through thoughts of losing her. Thoughts of having to bury her at twenty-five years old and living by myself creeped in. It was the first and one of the last times that I would really let doubt fully grab control of my mind. It was such a dark and empty place. Every inch of our apartment screamed memories of our great romance and life together. I broke down in the middle of our room. My parents came over and put their arms around me, and we sat there and cried for some time. Eventually, I gathered my stuff, left the note on the fridge untouched, and got back into the car.

As we got off the elevator back at the hospital, the main waiting room on the fourth floor looked like a homeless shelter. There were so many people with sleeping bags, blankets, and pillows. Their little areas had been turned into makeshift living quarters for long stays. I was happy to retreat to the secluded hallway closer to the actual ICU area where Lisa was.

I empathized with those who had other friends and families going through emergencies, but selfishly I wanted to be away from most people aside from our friends.

Not truly knowing what to say during times like this, people will reach for anything to try to bring comfort. Often it is in the form of some situational comparison to something their friend or family member once had or is currently going through. It has taught me a valuable lesson that I now try to implement when others are going through difficult trials. I often had the habit of trying to bring comfort to others in the same way, by discussing a friend or family member who faced similar difficulties. The intent in this is heartfelt, but in the moment, really all people want is for you to listen or be there. Their every ounce of energy and emotion is being slaughtered by the current state of their loved one, and the focus should not be taken from that. Sometimes it is OK to just say, "I am so sorry. I am here grieving with you through this." Sometimes it is OK to say nothing.

Most of our friends had gone home for the night. I can never adequately thank all those who walked through those hospital doors to go through those dark hours with us and our family. There is nothing like turning to see the face of someone who cares about you and will do anything for you in the midst of life-shattering events.

Lisa was in stable condition, and we would not know anything until the next day around midafternoon. It was a weird feeling knowing that life was continuing on as normal in the outside world while everything in mine was so disordered. People needed to go home to sleep for work the next day. Yet work was the last thing on my mind. I did not know if I would even go back at all that school year. Nor did I really care.

I cannot thank my coworkers, other coaches, and administration enough for the huge weight they took off my shoulders by taking on my different roles at school and picking up my slack. For that I am forever grateful to the Pioneer Heritage Middle School family.

The friends and family who were still around our makeshift waiting room continued to pray and draw encouragement from our faith in Christ. A community journal was being passed around so each person could express his or her feelings and write encouraging things for Lisa to read later. A few of them had started a CaringBridge website for Lisa. This was such a great help, and I was grateful they were taking on this role. My phone was beginning to blow up with messages and calls from people offering support and looking for information. It was overwhelming, so I just turned my phone on silent. Over the next couple of days, I left many draft messages unsent in my outbox because I would get sidetracked from answering people.

I will forever empathize with this aspect of people going through medical emergencies as well. It is beyond difficult, if not impossible, to update and keep people in the loop. The CaringBridge site took that pressure off me and allowed a central point of information for people to read about Lisa's situation as soon as something new developed. Thank you to our dear friends Jennie, Barbara, and Natalie who took on this role. They served and loved us so well in doing this. Their hope-filled words were beautiful and so important during that time. We are thankful we will have those words forever to remember our journey.

From that point on, I decided I was not going to let my fear and anxiety destroy my faith. I knew my God had a plan. I knew He was a God of miracles, and He was the ultimate healer. If I truly believed those things, and that everything in our lives was meant to bring Him ultimate glory, then I needed to shape up and start acting like it.

These are the times God promised we will have in this world. These are opportunities to test and strengthen our faith laid out for us in the book of James, opportunities for us to show why Jesus is worth it. This is why we can have hope in a hospital room even when all the odds are stacked against us, why we have faith like Abraham that even if our loved one is taken from us, our God has the power to bring him or her back to life.

If I could not have faith during this time, then how genuine was my faith in the first place? I desperately wanted to make God proud. From then on, with His help, I wanted to put that faith into practice.

Lisa's situation was getting worse by the minute, and it made me believe that God was setting the stage for the most epic miracle we could imagine. He was allowing the focus to be pulled so tightly on Him that only He could get the glory for what He was about to do.

I fought minute by minute and hour by hour to hold on to this truth. He restored and strengthened my faith in Him in that hospital hallway to a degree I cannot even describe. I prayed, "Lord, give me the strength to praise You in every situation and outcome from this point on. I pray that others will be brought closer to You through this situation and people will answer Your call on their lives. If even one person is changed through this, then it is worth it."

Psalms 3:3–5 describes perfectly this spiritual battle I had been dealing with: "But You, oh Lord, are a shield about me, my glory and the lifter of my head. I cried aloud to the Lord, and He answered me from His holy hill. I lay down and slept; I woke again, for the Lord sustained me."

I woke from a light sleep, crammed halfway onto a conference-room chair. It was time to take on another day. My wife was in there fighting for her life, and it was a fight all of us were determined to win.

Over the course of those hours that I spent in the ICU, I took notice of Lisa's "neighbor." I found out through his precious wife, Judy, that his name was Kris. Kris had been in the ICU for multiple weeks and was also in need of a liver transplant. During those next few days, Judy and I grew close. We found comfort in going through this similar trial together. It did not take long for me to see that Judy was also a Christian.

We spent time in prayer together, specifically praying for the transplant-board meeting that would take place later that afternoon. Kris's and Lisa's cases would be presented to the transplant board. We prayed Lisa's blood disease would not keep her from making the list, and we also prayed that Kris would not be denied reentry onto the list. He had had some complications while in the ICU that had led to him being taken off the list days earlier.

It was inspiring to see how Judy loved Kris so well. She spent sleepless hours at the hospital doing everything she could to help her husband fight this battle. What an example for other couples. I am grateful and can say I am better for knowing her.

Most of Wednesday, February 5, was a waiting game. Lisa was stable but ultimately dying. Those are such hard words to write, but it was our reality. People began showing up at the hospital again, and most of the late morning and afternoon was spent either by Lisa's side or visiting with the numerous members of Lisa's support group. Time seemed to pass so slowly. We waited with anxious anticipation for the transplant-committee meeting that would decide the fate of Lisa's case. We focused our energy in praying that she would not have an infection or blood disease that would keep her off of the transplant list.

Around three thirty the liver specialist turned the corner to meet us in the ICU hallway. He gave us the best-case news we so eagerly wanted to hear. Lisa was approved for a transplant and was going to be put on the list immediately! One step closer to survival. One step closer to a miracle. We all knew Lisa was a fighter. Every time Cheryl was by her bedside, she would beg Lisa to keep fighting. We were one round closer to her winning the fight. God was in her corner, and that was all she needed. We rejoiced that Kris was also approved to be put back on the list.

The liver specialist had mentioned Lisa needing a procedure done in order to buy her time until she could be transplanted. In this TIPS procedure, the radiologists would use guided imaging to tunnel through an entry point in Lisa's neck down to her liver. From there they would use a shunt to reroute her blood from the hepatic veins in her liver back to her heart. Before I knew it, it was go time. She was being prepped and was ready for her second big surgical procedure in the past two days. It seemed like it had been weeks since her gallbladder removal.

As I walked alongside my wife's bed being rolled toward the elevators to the next operating room, I began to grow anxious. She was not hooked up to the ventilation machine for this journey downstairs, and it felt like minutes passed before the nurse would give another squeeze to the handheld ventilator providing oxygen to her lungs. It was similar to that feeling you get when driving in a rainstorm and having that extended delay in between swipes of your windshield wipers. Just when you think you cannot see enough to drive any farther and feel like you need to take control, the next swipe occurs. So it seemed with his methodical pumps of air through her mouthpiece.

While taking the staff elevator toward the operating room, I got separated from our family and friends. I had no idea where I was in the hospital or how to direct them to my location if they called. I just hoped they would eventually find us.

I was able to kiss her on the forehead before one of the nurses led me into an empty waiting room. Here the business side came in, and he began going over the paperwork for her procedure with me. He began by telling me that it was a necessary surgery in order to give Lisa the best chance of making it to and through transplant. I still did not know how much time Lisa had left before it would be too late, and I was definitely too afraid to ask. He began listing off the numerous risks that accompanied this TIPS procedure. Uncontrollable bleeding, necessary transfusion, and death were a few that stuck out to me. My heart was racing one hundred miles an hour, and I could feel sweat forming on my brow. What happened next is something I will never forget for the rest of my life.

Midsentence, this man stopped, looked at me in my fear, and asked, "Can I pray with you?"

Wow! What an amazing God moment. It was another example of the Lord covering me in these difficult moments. Another reminder that He is surrounding us with a great cloud of believers whom He is allowing to participate in His work. It was such a comfort to sit in the empty waiting room and call out to our God with this nurse who was going to be assisting with Lisa's surgery. I thank the Lord for this guy's faithfulness, that seeing me in that moment would give him the courage and willingness to live out his faith in his workplace. I am forever grateful for the impact that he had on me that day. It is a constant reminder that prayer is so powerful. Community prayer radiates strength, and it encourages those who are weary. Thank you, God, for these mercies.

Shortly after I finished signing papers, the rest of the group made their way to the waiting room. The surgery was going to last anywhere from one to four hours. The room was mostly quiet in anticipation after we had another intense prayer session. So many people were there to offer support that the waiting room could not even hold us. Overflow began to form in the adjacent hallways. God has truly blessed us with a great support system. I can never repay everyone for keeping me so steadfast in Christ's truths during these hours of uncertainty. I will hold dear the memory of my dad, Rick, taking me to the chapel down the hall, wrapping his arms around me, and praying for my wife's healing.

After forty-five minutes, someone from our group pointed me in the direction of a doctor looking for me. I was so excited, thinking I would be getting an update about how the procedure was going.

"We are done, and she is doing fine. Everything went as well as expected."

What? I thought. They said it would take anywhere from one to four hours. Completely finished in well under the expected time frame. Only God could do that. I wish I had gotten that nurse's name who prayed with me before Lisa's surgery. What an answer to prayer.

I am pretty sure Lisa's dad and I did a chest bump with a little touchdown-like celebration in that hallway. "God's got this, my boy!" he said. "He is working miracles. I know she is going to make it. Our girl is a fighter!"

We had not made it out of danger yet, but God was leading us step by step. We were in the heart of a mountain range of challenges. Yet God had helped us reach a peak that night. After all He had already done, we were revitalized and saying, "On to the next one."

We were riding the high of a successful TIPS procedure for Lisa for the next couple of hours. We had made our way back to our little waiting room, and we spent some more time praising God and updating the next CaringBridge post. A woman appeared in professional dress and asked me to follow her. She led me into the ICU area, back past Lisa's room, and into an office. As we sat down at the desk, she made some small talk with me while she prepared a binder full of information. I noticed the words "Pretransplant Information" printed on the top.

Over the next five minutes, she flew through about a year's worth of information contained on those papers. This was a binder that patients received when they were put on the transplant list. It explained the scale for determining where people were placed on the list. The scores related directly to a mortality percentage. The higher the score, the higher up you moved on the list. In other words, the sickest people with the greatest risk of dying were at the top. However, this could change daily or hourly.

In Lisa's case it was explained to me that she would be listed as a status-1A patient. Status-1A patients jumped directly to the top of the list because they had sudden- and severe-onset liver failure. This meant, based on her status, Lisa had a life expectancy of hours to a couple of days without a transplant. Praise God this lady did not fill me in on this detail, and it was not until later that I truly found out and understood what her life expectancy was. She explained to me that when a liver became available, one of the surgeons from Baylor Dallas would travel to the donor's location to inspect and recover the organ. The coordinator at that time would give me enough information about the donor and organ, and then it would be my decision to accept or reject the liver. *Wow, so I will have to choose whether to take it or, if it does not feel right, risk waiting for a better organ?*

I began to worry about how I would choose the "right" liver for Lisa, and God spoke to me loud and clear in that moment of anxiety: "I will provide the perfect liver. Do you think I would leave such a crucial piece to this puzzle and My glory in your hands?"

God was right. He would make that crystal clear. It wouldn't even be a decision. The liver He would provide would be perfect.

"Sit back, and praise My name, Reid. That is all you need to do. I've got this!"

The coordinator finished her presentation that felt like a crash course in the transplantation process, I signed a few papers, and she told me that another coordinator would call me when they had a liver.

"How long will that be?" I asked.

"There is no way of knowing for sure, but with her being top priority, it should happen pretty fast. If she had to wait three days, I would be shocked," she added.

I took the binder with me and, with my head spinning, made my way back to the family waiting room.

Now all we could do was pray and wait. Not long after our conversation, most of our friends and some family headed home to get some sleep. We were pretty sure things would be uneventful at least for a day or two, so I told everyone we would let them know if we heard anything.

My parents had gotten a hotel room at the hospital, and, finally, around one thirty in the morning, they cajoled me into going to sleep up there for a few hours. Lisa's mom, Cheryl, and our friend Jennie were going to take turns sitting with Lisa in the ICU.

The nurses, seeing how exhausted I was, encouraged me to start getting rest. "Lisa is going to need you much more after her transplant. You need to get sleep while she is resting. She is going to need her husband after her surgery."

That was enough for me. I hugged everyone who was still there, and my parents and I began the winding trek through the hospital to the hotel room.

We were not even two minutes into our walk to the room when my cell phone began to ring. It was our friend Barbara, who had been in the waiting room moments ago. As I began to answer it, Cheryl was calling me at the same time. My heart was about to jump out of my chest. I had a feeling about this call. It was as if God was giving me a big bear hug. With shaking fingers, I hit the green "Answer Call" button.

Cheryl's voice came through with a tone of shock and excitement. "Reid...they have a liver!"

Was this a dream? How cruel if I was about to wake up in that hotel-room bed. This was no dream, just another answered prayer.

I turned, looked at my parents, and said, "They have a liver—they have one." I gave them a big hug and all but sprinted through those halls back toward the ICU.

As I approached Cheryl, she pointed toward Lisa's ICU pod and told me someone was waiting on the phone for me. I picked up that phone and talked to the transplant coordinator, who confirmed to me that they had a liver for Lisa. During this conversation, and throughout the transplant process, confidential details were protected. The coordinator was able to tell me only that it was a young, healthy liver. The donor was a fifteen-year-old female. In that moment of relief and gratefulness, those last words ripped me apart. I fought back tears of joy for Lisa but even more for the heartache that this other family must be going through.

"Mr. Barker, do you have any other questions as this time?"

I know I had millions, but I could not think straight. "No" was the only answer I could muster up. Before we ended our conversation, she told me that she would call me again in a little while to go over a few more things. "Thank you," I said and hung up the phone.

I spent a few moments in the room with Lisa before heading back to the waiting room. I know the nurses were thrilled for us as well. We had all grown close to them during our long days, and they had become like our personal cheer squad. These were the moments I was sure they worked hard for. They had done their job so well. They had used their God-given gifts and love to sustain Lisa's life until she could be transplanted.

Our family was obviously excited and anxious to hear the news, even if I did not have a lot of details yet. We circled up in that room once again, this time lifting up the family whose lives were drastically changed in the recent days or hours. When we were done, I pulled a chair up near the ICU double doors, waiting for another phone call. The hospital was quiet, and the hours ticked by with no call.

The adrenaline that was a direct result of the life-changing news of an available organ wore off, and my eyes grew more and more heavy with each minute. Finally, around four thirty, another call from the coordinator came through. She explained that Lisa would be transplanted later that day. She obviously had not originally been scheduled for surgery, but they would be working her in. Once the organ was recovered, there was only about a twelve-hour window to transplant it into Lisa. She estimated a surgery start time around nine thirty that morning.

Unbelievable. We had already seen miracles performed in those few days, but this one was just incredible. A mere ten hours since being placed at the top of the transplant list, Lisa had an available organ. That was just unheard of. That was ten hours at the time we were notified. I am sure the matching and process of that liver going to Lisa began even earlier.

After calling friends and family who had left earlier that night to let them know Lisa was getting transplanted later that morning, I headed to bed at five thirty. I was near delirium and needed to get a couple hours of sleep if I wanted to make it through that day. I was overwhelmed by God's grace and mercy. Today was the day. Lisa was getting a second chance at life. I knew God was going to do great things through His story for her life. I lay down, set my alarm, and drifted into a light sleep.

CHAPTER 5

FEBRUARY 6, 2014

Reid

The idea of organ donation and transplantation blows my mind. The fact that God created the human body in such a way that a gift from a donor can be recovered, placed in, and reconnected in another living human being is nothing short of miraculous. I want to take a moment to focus on that gift of life.

It is extremely difficult to explain the emotions that I felt as the husband of a soon-to-be transplant patient. Of course, more than anything, I had begged and pleaded with God to save Lisa's life, all the while knowing that ultimately the only way for Lisa's life to be spared, barring complete healing of her liver syndrome, would be for someone else to pass away. This was tough to swallow, but I tried to focus on the perfection of God's ultimate plan throughout this whole thing. Never was God taken by surprise through any of this. From the moment we found out they had a liver for Lisa, we began praying for that fifteen-year-old girl's family. My heart ached for them, and we prayed vigorously for God to cover them in the peace and comfort that only He can provide. I found comfort in the fact that Lisa was a registered organ donor herself. She would not be accepting a gift that she had not already demonstrated willingness to give herself. Still, it is always difficult to rejoice in the moment knowing someone else is experiencing the deepest of sorrows.

I woke up the morning of February 6, 2014, with an even stronger sense of hope and faith. It was about seven thirty when my alarm went off—a mere two hours after I had finally gone to bed, after talking to the transplant coordinator for the last time early that morning. Never could I have imagined they would have a liver so quickly. God had pulled me tightly into His arms over the last twenty-four hours, and I cried out to Him that morning for His name to be glorified that day. I knew how many people were invested in offering their support, prayers, and love. For Lisa to go from seemingly perfectly healthy to hours from death shortly after set the stage for only God's name to be lifted up. The story was reaching its climax. He had brought her too far to let her story end here.

The morning of February 6, 2014, the prettiest snow was falling over much of North Texas. I was the first one from our group to be awake and walking around the hospital. When I got down to the ICU, the double doors of Lisa's room were shut. Outside I reread the posted sign that said something about waiting until the doors were open to enter. The automatic doors to the hallway opened, and one of the transplant surgeons walked out. He said that if everything went as planned, they would start prepping her for surgery around nine thirty. I thanked him again and headed to Lisa's room.

I remember holding her swollen hand and telling her that today was the day she was getting a new liver. It was possibly, in all reality, the last day I would spend with my wife. This was another risky surgery and one that had to be extremely difficult. I am still amazed at how many moving parts come together seamlessly to make such an incredible event possible.

A major transition began to take place in my mind that morning. Not only was I thinking about Lisa's surgery and survival, but for the first time, I began contemplating life for her, and us, after the transplant. If, God willing, she did make it through surgery, would things be normal again for us? There had been mention of possible brain damage from swelling and being intubated for that time. Would she even remember me? To what extreme was this going to cause emotional and mental stress on her? Was she going to freak out when she saw the size of the scar? Would we be able to have kids? What about the fifteen-year-old girl? Lisa was going to be crushed when she found out she was alive because someone so young had lost her life. She was so firmly grounded in her faith before this...would she be bitter at God?

As quickly as these thoughts entered my consciousness, God laid upon my heart these two verses: Matthew 6:34 says, "Therefore do not be anxious about tomorrow, for tomorrow will be anxious for itself. Sufficient for the day is its own trouble." Philippians 4:6 says, "Do not be anxious about anything, but in everything by prayer and supplication with thanksgiving let your requests be made known to God."

Such simple truth in these words. God was saying, *Reid, why waste your time worrying about the troubles of tomorrow? You should be using that energy to support your wife, praise My name for answered prayers, and continue to pray for the events of today.*

If the last few days had taught me anything, it was confirming the truth that we are not promised tomorrow. It sounds so simple and is a phrase we throw around so often. Yet if you really sit back and think, it puts everything in perfect perspective. We are called to live in the moment. God has orchestrated our lives to the most minute timetable. He strategically gave us those seconds in every minute of every hour of every day of our lives. They are all meant for one thing—to spend worshipping Jesus in all we do. It is so easy for us to get distracted with the events of tomorrow, and, consequently, we miss out on participating with God today. I urge each of us to stay focused on living in the present moment, because it is the only moment that truly matters.

I could see the snow falling outside Lisa's ICU pod window and spent a few minutes describing to her how beautiful this scene was. Never in my wildest dreams did it occur to me that this seemingly beautiful weather could possibly cause issues with her new organ arriving on time to Dallas.

As things began to stir around the hospital, and family and friends began making their way back up there, our anxiety with the weather grew. They were delayed in preparing Lisa by about two hours, but I do not think it was due to the weather. I think they had to work her into an operating room with the schedule that had already been set prior to the night before. Still, even with the delay, things started to come together, and the time was drawing near.

Finally, it was time. Lisa had been prepped over the last couple of hours and was about to be wheeled down for her lifesaving surgery. I kissed her forehead again and told her I loved her and would see her after surgery. That was the hardest "see you later" of our time together. I knew this surgery was going to give her a new chance at life. We were told it would last anywhere from four to ten hours. I honestly was more nervous the night before waiting for the TIPS procedure than I was making my way to the transplant waiting room. As each new challenge had arisen, God had performed miracle after miracle to sustain Lisa. I believed he would do the same in seeing her through this surgery and recovery.

Our group of fifteen or so set up camp in the waiting room, and I made my way over to the surgery-update screen. I found Lisa's surgery number and was shocked to see the visual representation of a four-to-ten-hour surgery through the length of a color-coded bar.

Finally, that bar changed color, and Lisa's surgery began at 1:58 p.m. I was completely exhausted, so I found the nearest couch, covered up with a blanket, and tried to rest. At 3:20 p.m. my phone began to ring and vibrate on my chest. I knew this was the operating room calling to give me an update on Lisa. My mouth was dry, and I could barely conjure up a nervous "Hello."

"Is this Mr. Barker? I just wanted to let you know that everything is going as planned in here with Lisa."

I released the breath I had been holding. What a relief. We had made it to another peak. I could not lie down anymore. My adrenaline had picked up after that update. I spent the rest of the time with friends and family, talking about anything and everything to stay distracted.

Some time passed before the next call came at 5:01 p.m. "Everything still looks good, and we should be finishing up soon."

We could see the finish line. Another peak.

A very short half hour later, at 5:30 p.m., I received the final call. "They're closing Lisa up."

I hung up the phone and screamed an echo of her words. *Thank You, Jesus. Thank You for covering her through this.*

Only a couple of minutes after receiving the final call, Lisa's transplant surgeons walked into the waiting room. They had this quiet, humble confidence about them. I had not formally met either of them before, but it took everything for me to not run up and wrap my arms around the two of them. They had just aided in giving my wife new life. The assistant surgeon explained to us that Lisa had done great, and the next twenty-four to forty-eight hours were crucial. As they were about to leave, I thanked them and shook both their hands. Hands that had just placed a new, life-giving organ into my wife—a precious gift that a family had willingly given in their deepest sorrow so that someone else could live.

Lisa's total surgery time had been a mere three hours and twenty-one minutes. Another surgery well shorter than the aforementioned time estimate. To some this may seem like a small thing, but to us it was just more evidence of God's sovereignty. It was another example of Him strengthening our faith during this trial. All our family and friends circled up in that waiting room, held hands, and praised God for His miracle. After our prayer we stood there singing "How Great Is Our God." We wanted there to be no doubt about Whom we found our hope in.

About an hour after Lisa's liver transplant, I sneaked out of the waiting room and walked down the hall to a quiet corner. I had not been able to sit down and write in her community journal. It's not that I did not want to; I just could not find the right words to say. I began to cry as I thought about how proud I was of Lisa and her fight. I decided this was a moment I wanted to document and share with her later. In that quiet hospital corner, I pulled out my phone, opened the camera app, and hit record.

"Hey, baby, it's about an hour after your liver-transplant surgery, and I am just overwhelmed by the Lord's grace. I know you're going to get through this. I know that. I just can't wait to kiss you and to hug you. It's been overwhelming, scary, terrifying, but also the most comforting experience of my life. I have never felt closer to God. I have never felt more in love with you. I just want you to know that we are going to get through this. We are going to fight because you have fought so hard this week, and I am so proud of you. I love you so much. I'm just here watching, waiting for you to recover. Can't wait to see you, and I love you. Proud to call you my wife."

The next twenty-four to forty-eight hours were critical. We were not out of the woods yet, but it almost seemed as if we were. Lisa had survived a liver-transplant surgery! Her body would almost instantly recognize this new organ as foreign, and her young immune system would begin attacking it. This same system that is at war on a daily basis to keep our bodies functioning properly against bacteria and other toxic things would treat this new liver the same way. Thankfully, due to modern medicine, Lisa would be on anti-rejection medicine for the rest of her life. This medicine would suppress that war machine known as the immune system enough to allow her new liver to work in harmony with her body.

This situation so closely parallels the Christian existence. We were created to live and work in conjunction with God. Yet sin separates us from His perfection and causes us not to live in that harmony with Him. Still, out of His perfect love and mercy, God sent His son, Jesus, to die for our sins. He is our anti-rejection medication. He is the necessary formula for our God to recognize us. Without Him we die, but with Him we are able to live a life of abundance. It is a prescription we all need and one that we can all afford because Jesus paid that price for us. No copay or deductible is necessary. All you have to do is accept it. Choose to live a life of abundance today. Choose Jesus!

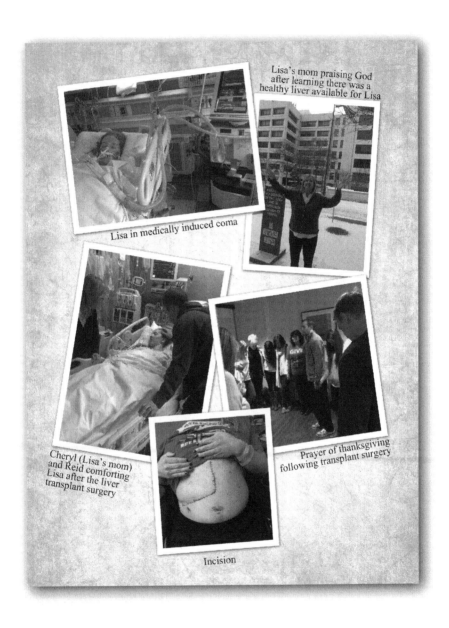

Lisa's mom praising God after learning there was a healthy liver available for Lisa

Lisa in medically induced coma

Cheryl (Lisa's mom) and Reid comforting Lisa after the liver transplant surgery

Prayer of thanksgiving following transplant surgery

Incision

CHAPTER 6

THE AWAKENING

Reid

Friday morning I could not wait to get into the ICU to be with Lisa. Cheryl had stayed up most of the night to be with her so that I could be rested when she woke up. They would be taking her off intubation soon. I had such an intense nervousness for the approaching moment. I was so worried about what her mental state would be like when she woke up. Would she know what was going on? Would she remember having her gallbladder taken out? Would she even know who I was? The effects of the medication could be minimal or severe. Only time would tell.

As the doctor was preparing to remove Lisa's breathing tube, he asked me to step outside because he said it could be a little disturbing watching him take her off the machine. I appreciated the heads-up, and I did not want to witness another uncomfortable event for my wife. I had seen and lived through plenty of them over the past few days, and I was so tired of watching her body be pushed to the extremes. From the hallway, I could hear the machine being removed and then shut off in the room.

Shortly after that, I was able to come back in. I felt myself awaken from an oxygen-deprived trance in which I had been holding my own breath while watching to make sure Lisa would breathe on her own. Her breathing was not as strong as it normally would be, but they said it would strengthen quickly. For the first time in more than three days, I bent over and gave my wife a kiss. Her lips were chapped from having her mouth open for multiple days, but I do not know that I have ever shared a sweeter kiss with my wife.

The process of her coming off the medication seemed to happen pretty quickly. I asked the nurse if he thought she could hear me now, and he said, "Yes, watch this. Mrs. Lisa, can you hear me?"

I saw the faintest movement in her face, but it was definitely her acknowledging his voice.

I grabbed her hand and began talking to her over the next couple of minutes. Excitedly, I told her, "Baby, if you can hear me, squeeze my hand."

It was not strong, but I felt the pressure of her fingers intensify around my own. My heart was about to beat out of my chest. That was the same hand that I had held in the chapel on July 6, 2012, and vowed to hold forever. Her same hand that had placed a ring on my finger, acknowledging her commitment to us. Yes, that faint squeeze of my hand solidified we were still Team Barker. Thank You, God! She was now awake.

Lisa

Confused. Scared. Uncomfortable. Worried. These were just some of the many emotions I experienced when my eyes opened for the first time. My ears were flooded with loud, unfamiliar sounds. I could sense movement around me, but I was too afraid to move. I subconsciously remember my intubation tube being removed. It felt like my entire body was being suctioned up.

My body felt encapsulated. My neck was stiff and felt immovable due to the weight of the cords I could see coming out of the right side. Out of my peripheral vision, I could see blood flowing through those tubes. My eyes began to scan my surroundings. I was in a confined space surrounded on two sides by a curtain.

Where am I? The thoughts ran through my head, but they could not be transformed into audible words. I had so much I wanted to say, but I had no power in my voice to make any sound. My throat hurt, and I was so thirsty. My tongue literally felt raw. I would soon come to realize that my last full meal and drink of water were on January 31, 2014, and it was now February 7. It later became apparent that I was going to have to relearn how to use my vocal cords and how to swallow.

Reid

Over the next hour or so, Lisa became more cognizant as she drifted in and out of sleep. She would kind of nod and acknowledge our presence more and more as time ticked by. Cheryl had joined us in the room, and we spent those sweet moments of her waking all together. Suddenly, in a whisper that could barely be heard, Lisa said my name. Unsure if I had really heard it or not, I looked at her in a confused way, trying to get her to repeat it again.

"Reid!" she said in a quiet tone, but definitely clear this time.

My eyes caught hers, and she uttered the first phrase in three days.

"Reid, what the hell is going on?" She had a fearful and inquisitive look in her eyes.

I glanced over at Cheryl, and we both had dumbfounded looks on our faces. Lisa never cusses, so it was somewhat comical, aside from the reality of the situation, to hear those be the first words out of her mouth. I confirmed with Cheryl, "Did she really just say that?" That was definitely her first phrase, and one that we still laugh about to this day.

The next twenty-four hours were filled with us trying to nurture her to a place where she would be able to wrap her mind around the severity of the situation. I did not know how much she knew or remembered. She was emotional on the different medications she was on and very forgetful. She must have asked me one hundred times where she was and if she was dying. All I knew was that now was not the time to reveal to her that she had had a liver transplant. That time would come eventually, but I did not know exactly when. All we could do now was love on her and be there for her.

Lisa

I was having horrific nightmares coming off of the sedation drugs and was having a really hard time separating the nightmares from reality. Every few minutes I would ask my family, "Am I dying?"

They would always calmly answer with a smile, "No, you are going to be just fine."

I did not believe at the time that I was going to be OK. I would try to close my eyes to rest, and then I would have more vivid nightmares. That first day I did not want to close my eyes because I was scared to fall asleep and go back into that darkness. The content of those satanic nightmares was so terrifying that I remember thinking, *Jesus, I am ready if You want to take me now.*

Every noise and beep continued to startle me. My dialysis machine kept acting up, and nurses were constantly in and out trying to fix it. Reid and my mom played it off well, but I know they got really nervous every time that machine had problems.

I woke up thinking I had only had my gallbladder removed. I remember my mom and sister at the foot of my bed and my sister telling me that my CaringBridge site already had over ten thousand views and that many people were praying for me.

CaringBridge site? Why in the world do I have a CaringBridge site? Wow, this must have been serious, I thought as I was in shock. It really frustrated me that everyone else knew what was going on with me, but I did not. CaringBridge was for people who were going through major, life-altering events concerning their health. I'd only had my gallbladder removed. That was a routine surgery. Or so I previously thought. *People from all over are praying for me? Wait, what? Why do I need all these prayers? What has happened?*

My best friend, Lauren Desai, walked into my room. As she came walking into my ICU pod, I remember thinking, *I really am dying.* Why else would she have flown in from California? She was here to tell me good-bye. Then our dear friends Drake and Jenna Thornton from Corpus Christi came in, and another friend, Ashley Hann, from Nebraska. *This is it. I am dying.* It never crossed my mind at the time that our remarkable friends had traveled there to support me and my family and to love on us and to pray over us and for us.

Reid and other family members took turns sitting with me in the ICU during the day. My sweet mother would come in and take over part of the night shift so Reid could get some sleep. I would softly whisper "ice chips" to her, and she would feed me ice chips to quench my thirst. This would last about two minutes, and I would ask for them again. When she was standing, she would quietly run her hands through my hair—something she used to do when I was little to get me to fall asleep.

I remember so clearly her sitting in the chair next to my bed just watching me. Sometimes I would look over, and she would have drifted off to sleep. I could see on her face how much she had been through that week and how concerned she was for her baby girl.

Someone had mentioned to my mom that listening to music in the ICU can help calm a patient's fears. My mom decided to try this. She pulled up Pandora Radio on her iPhone and turned it to Kari Jobe radio. She knew Kari Jobe was my favorite Christian artist. She laid the phone on my shoulder, and she noticed there was an immediate change in my demeanor. My face went from being stressed and having a look of hurt and fear to being calm and at peace. I listened to Kari's music, and the words put me at ease. Even though I still did not fully understand what was going on or what had happened the past week, the lyrics in her songs reminded me that God is in control, and He had me in the palm of His hand.

I also heard the song "Oceans," by Hillsong United, and it brought me so much comfort and hope. I would listen to this song and think about Peter being on the water with Jesus and Jesus reaching out His hand to Peter and saying, "Trust Me!" *Wow.* I vividly remember picturing myself standing on water with Jesus and just hearing Him say, "Lisa, keep your eyes on Me, reach for My hand, and trust Me, My precious daughter."

In the middle of the night, our dear friend Jennie Watkins would come and relieve my mom so she could go get a few hours of sleep on the uncomfortable chairs in the hospital waiting area. Jennie would then take over and listen for my soft whispers of "ice chips." It was clear to me that my family and friends were rock stars who selflessly gave up sleep and their needs to take care of mine.

As I became more aware in the ICU, it was actually refreshing to see familiar faces. One night my general surgeon from Baylor Plano, who had removed my gallbladder, came to visit me. This was such a sweet surprise. I could not believe that a busy surgeon would take time out of her schedule not only to come check on me and my family, but to bring her husband to meet me as well. She was eight months pregnant at the time, and to everyone's surprise, I remembered her due date and recited it to her when she entered the ICU. This was remarkable because I could hardly remember anything from the previous few days, but that date stuck out to me from when she had told me it on Monday.

It meant the world to me that she was so invested in my condition. I am so thankful she was so thorough and noticed there was a problem with my liver. I recognize that not all surgeons would have been as diligent as she was. She had stayed up all night Monday researching my liver disease and talking to the hepatologist who would soon take care of me. Reid and I have kept in touch with her, and she reminds me that I nearly caused her to go into early labor that week. We are so thankful for the relationship we have with her. She was a godsend for my family that week as she ultimately saved my life from night one.

I do not remember many of my nurses from the first few days of my stay in the ICU as I was sedated, but the first night nurse I do remember was Anne. She was my nurse the night I woke up from my coma. She was so great and very patient with me. I remember not being able to sleep one night, and she had mentioned that at four that morning, she was going to give me a sponge bath. I eagerly watched the clock and waited to finally feel refreshed. I had not bathed in a week. I was always a very modest person before all of this occurred, but when you have to allow other people to completely care for you, it humbles you very quickly.

Many of the nurses were surprised at how much I kept thanking them after my shots and when they would give me medicine or do anything for me. This must be unusual for patients to do, especially if they are not feeling well, but to me they were saving my life with everything they did for me, and I wanted them to know they were appreciated and how grateful I was for their help.

I remember lying in my ICU bed one night, looking up over my curtain in my room, and seeing flashes of the Winter Olympics on the TV hanging from the ceiling in the hallway. I thought, *The Olympics have started. What day is it? I missed the opening ceremonies?* I quickly began replaying in my head all the activities I had scheduled for the last week and how much I had missed, such as birthday parties and our dear friend's wedding shower. I had just lost a week of my life.

Sunday, February 9, was the first day I fully remember. A different doctor, whom I had not seen before, walked into my ICU pod and asked Reid if they had told me what had happened yet. Reid kindly told her that they were waiting to explain everything until I was more aware of my surroundings. Up until this point, every few minutes, I had still been asking where I was and if I was going to live.

This doctor came to the right side of my bed and laid it all out there for me. "Well, you went into acute kidney, liver, and, eventually, respiratory failure. You were flown from Baylor Plano to Baylor Dallas. You developed a rare liver condition called Budd–Chiari, which only one in a million people develop. Your Budd–Chiari was caused by an undiagnosed blood disease. You are on a continuous kidney-dialysis machine and have had a liver transplant." She then compassionately said, "Do you have any questions?"

I softly said no, but my mind was thinking yes. I did not even know where to start.

I turned my head gently to the right and looked at the dialysis machine. I had learned about dialysis in dental-hygiene school and how to treat patients who were on it, but I could not believe that at twenty-five years old, I was now the patient in need of dialysis.

After she left, my family rushed to my bed to comfort me. I could tell they were all waiting to see how I was going to respond. I just remember thinking, *Everyone already knew this? Everyone knows, and I am just now finding out.* I wished I had been prepared for this going into it. I wished I had known I was going to need a transplant.

Those were my initial feelings, but I would later realize it was a blessing in disguise that I was unaware of my need for a new organ. A provision from God. I honestly never really reacted to finding out about the transplant. I just had more of an attitude like, *OK, what do we do now?* I knew I was in survival mode and had learned how crucial the next few days, weeks, and months were going to be. I knew, at this point, I had to continue fighting hard for my life.

One evening another nurse came into my ICU pod and told me something that would calm my nerves. She told me that she had also been diagnosed with my liver condition, Budd–Chiari, when she was nineteen. She had had to have a liver transplant and was now in her fifties and doing great. That was such a comfort to me. I had no idea how long I could live with a new liver, and for her to be doing so great many years later was reassuring for me. It gave me and my family a little bit of hope that was so desperately needed.

My family told me about all of the visitors who had come to the hospital just to be near them, to give them hugs, to bring dinners. People I had not seen in years. I was blown away by the kindness of others and by the love we were shown. I loved hearing about our family and friends lining the hospital hallways and taking over the conference rooms near the ICU to pray together and to pray over me.

An ICU nurse would later tell me, "Your friends and family were just sitting there for hours."

Yes, they were sitting, but they were together as the Body of Christ, lifting me up before our precious Lord and Savior. "For where two or three are gathered in my name, there am I among them" (Matthew 18:20).

By Sunday night it had become clear to me that God was not ready for me yet. It was apparent that I had a purpose for staying on this earth. That purpose was to glorify and honor Him with the testimony He had just given me.

CHAPTER 7

IN THE MIDST OF THE STORM

Lisa

I remember that Monday morning well. So much was going on that many times it was almost overwhelming. It seemed like every couple of minutes, new doctors, nurses, family members, or visitors were at my bedside. I did not sleep much the night before, as I was anxiously anticipating my sponge bath from my nurse. The morning rolled around quickly, and the transplant team and residents were making their rounds in the ICU. I remember hearing talks that I could possibly come off dialysis if my numbers were improving. It seemed like the doctors just kept coming by and saying everything was improving, but I was not being taken off of anything.

Finally, the transplant surgeon came in and said those words that I had been waiting to hear: "You can come off dialysis today."

I still could not talk well, but with my raspy voice, I just said, "Thank you!"

The dialysis port would be staying in my neck for the remainder of my stay at the hospital because if my numbers did not keep improving, they would have to start me on dialysis again. I dreaded keeping the tubes in, but at least they would not be attached to anything, for now.

I also softly asked the surgeon when I would be able to drink water. The night before, I had seen my mom drinking a bottle of water. She was turned, trying to drink it out of my sight, but I happened to see, and I remember feeling so jealous that she could drink water. I felt as if I could drink an entire swimming pool if given the chance. It had been more than a week since I had drunk or eaten anything myself.

I will never forget him saying, "I think it would be fine for you to start a liquid diet. Someone get the girl some ice water." Those were by far the best words. It seemed like it took the ICU nurse hours to get me my water. My family had to explain to me that the part of the ICU I was in was one where a nurse had to be with the four patients in my pod 24-7. So she could not go get me water until another nurse could cover for her.

Eventually I had the cup in my hand, and with eagerness I thought I was going to guzzle that water down. I took one sip and was shocked. I was surprised that it hurt to drink, and even more than that, I had a hard time swallowing. Being intubated for that period of time caused my throat muscles to atrophy from lack of use. It took a bit of time, but gradually they started to come back, and drinking became easier.

They brought me in a tray of liquid foods to start eating. Reid started feeding me, and then my sweet sister, Laura, and my dad finished feeding me. I had Jell-O and remember that it felt so good on my throat because it was cold, but it hurt to swallow at the same time. Then I remember my stomach starting to gurgle and quickly becoming upset. I was so embarrassed because I had a catheter in and was having to just go to the bathroom in my bed. This is humiliating when you are only twenty-five years old. When you have to give up control and allow someone else to do everything for you, you quickly throw all modesty out the window. My family had to remind me that my body had to adjust to having food and liquid in it again. I had been so anxious to drink and eat, and it was such a disappointment for me.

The transplant surgeon also gave us some great news that Monday morning. I would finally be moving up to the fourteenth floor at Baylor Dallas. The fourteenth floor is the abdominal-transplant floor. We were so excited. I was anxious to be in my own room and to not have to hear so many sounds coming from every direction in the ICU. They told me it would be a while until a room was ready for me. It was a much longer day than I had hoped for. I rested for most of the day while my family took turns sitting with me. For some reason that day, I felt like I was somewhere different from where I had been lying for the past couple of days. I do not know how to explain it, but in my mind it was like I had been moved somewhere else. My family reassured me this was not the case.

Late afternoon, I still had not been moved upstairs. My dad kept checking on the situation, and they reassured us that they would move me as soon as they could. Reid was with me when we got a surprise visitor. One of my patients from the dental office I work at had stopped by to see me. I remember just having the biggest smile on my face and being so surprised that he took the time to come visit me. He is a pastor and has been a huge encouragement to me the last couple of years, especially with Reid and me getting married and through family prayer requests. He was able to pray with Reid and me that afternoon. I was starting to realize how many people were invested in our story. God was moving in powerful ways even while I was lying in a hospital bed. I have learned that some of God's best work is done in hospital beds and in sickness.

While I was resting, I remember a physical therapist and an occupational therapist coming in to see me. The occupational therapist asked if I could touch my head with my hands. I must have looked at her with a dumbfounded look on my face. *Yes, of course I can touch my head,* I was thinking. To my surprise, when I tried this, I could hardly lift my arms two inches from my bed. I was stunned. How could this be? I had just done a body-pump weight-lifting class at our gym last week. I was strong. They had me try to sit up in bed, and it took two people to help me sit up straight. It would be a while before my abs, which were cut through in surgery to allow access for my transplant, would be healed. My body felt like a complete noodle that I was no longer in control over. This was the first time I realized the possible recovery I was in for.

I began asking my family more questions as I became more aware of what was happening. I would ask them to take me back to Monday and Tuesday of the previous week and explain to me again how this all had happened. Poor Reid must have told me the same things a million times. My memory was so cloudy after being under anesthesia three times in four days, and I was not remembering things even after they had been told to me numerous times. Reid never got frustrated with me. He would just smile and start the story over again.

Some of my favorite stories I heard from family were about our friends who came to visit who may not usually be exposed to Christianity, prayer time, church, worship, and the like. I just love how God knows what people need at the perfect times. He strategically placed each person there that week who needed to be exposed to His goodness—those who needed to see that miracles did not just happen in the Bible, but they still happen today. These were friends and family who needed to see that God is worthy of being praised in the middle of a huge storm. This brought my soul so much joy to think of how God did this. From that Monday on, I kept saying, "If one person has become closer to God or has even come to know God through what has happened to me, then it has all been worth it."

A new ICU nurse for that day was prepping me to leave the ICU. She was changing me and changing my dressings on my incision. When she started to change the dressing on my stomach, I asked if I could see it. I was thinking that I still had four little incisions from the laparoscopic gallbladder removal. My stomach was not in much pain at that point, but when I looked down and saw staples across the majority of the center and right side of my stomach, my jaw dropped. I looked at Reid with the most frantic look on my face. I had thirty-two staples, starting from right under my breastbone in the middle of my stomach down to almost my belly button and then all the way across my stomach to my right side. It looked as if someone had opened me up halfway and then zipped me back up. From that point on, I felt pain. I was beginning to realize how big a surgery I'd had and how major this event truly was.

Finally, around six o'clock Monday evening, I was wheeled out of the ICU. My family was with me, and when we rounded the corner headed to the elevators, our dear friends Linda and Rusty Simpson and Barbara Graves were there recording my ride, cheering, and praising that I was out of the ICU. In the video they took, you can hear me softly saying, "I am so excited."

I made it to the fourteenth floor, and there was a nurse who greeted us as soon as we got off the elevator. Her name was Brittany. She looked around my age, and I was so thankful to see someone who could possibly relate to me. She told us she was not supposed to be working that night, but she was picking up a shift for someone. Little did we know how blessed we would be that she picked up that extra shift that day. Brittany was a godsend for us.

Brittany got us all settled in, and we were shocked by the room I had. It was huge. Reid said you could see the Dallas skyline out the windows and told me how beautiful it was. My brother gave me the best surprise that night when he brought our sweet nephew Jackson up to the hospital to see me. Jackson was wearing a shirt that said, "Best day ever," and we all could not agree more. I was out of the ICU. Definitely not out of the woods, but it was a huge step in the right direction, and that made it the best day ever.

Jennie and Reid both decided to stay with me that first night on the fourteenth floor. One slept on a chair to the left of me and the other across the room on the pullout bed. The rest of my family had gone home to get some much-needed rest now that my condition was a little more stable. I remember telling them how quiet it was in my room. I could still hear noises from other rooms and sometimes would think, *Why can't they just shut that machine up?* We started winding down for bed, and the nurses had put a pulse oximeter on my finger. It lit up red. We all got settled in bed, and I lifted my finger and said, "If y'all need me, I have my night-light on over here." I felt like E.T. Reid and Jennie busted out in laughter, and I chuckled for the first time since surgery. It hurt so bad to laugh, but I could tell they needed the laughter, and it did my soul good, too.

They both said, "Lisa is back."

One of the sweet techs had to come in every couple of hours throughout the night to help me to the restroom. I would press the nurse-call button, and she was there in seconds to help me. My catheter was now out, and I was in control of using the bathroom. She would have to help me out of my bed, let me bear hug her, and practically drag me to the restroom. My stomach was so upset. I had started my menstrual cycle because of all the shock my body was under the past week, and I had a leak in my groin where my original dialysis port was. This meant that every time I got up to use the restroom, my panties were soaked and had to be changed. Remember throwing modesty out the window? Realizing that I had to have a stranger help wipe me because I was too weak to do it myself was tough on me. She had to help me off the toilet because there was no way I could muster up enough strength to get up on my own. I remember on the way to the restroom that night looking up and catching a glimpse of myself in the mirror. Whoa, I looked like I had been through a rough week. She would get me back in the bed after the bathroom trips, and I would be completely wiped out. I felt like I had just run a few miles. It was an exhausting experience.

The nights were rough. I was so uncomfortable. I had always liked to sleep on my stomach before my surgery. Now I was forced to sleep on my back, and it was tough for me. The nurses kept adjusting me to make sure my back and bottom did not develop sores. I remember lying in bed just crying because I was so uncomfortable. The high doses of steroids I was on were causing me to have night sweats. I would become so hot and strip the blankets off myself and then get so cold and need them all back on minutes later. One of my precious night nurses, Lauren, had the idea to put ice packs on me to help me sleep. She gave me a sleeping pill, and between that and the ice packs, I was able to sleep for a few hours. I could have slept longer, but starting at six in the morning, the lab techs were there to draw blood, and it was time to start taking a handful of medications. My days were so long with respiratory therapy, physical and occupational therapy, doctor rotations with the transplant team, and numerous doctor visits that my rest was very scarce throughout the day.

Tuesday morning started my "busy days." It felt like I was at kids' camp where my whole daily agenda was planned out for me, and I had no say in it. Respiratory therapy was up first.

They would come in and have me do breathing treatments. I would be lying if I told you I enjoyed these sessions. I dreaded seeing them three times a day. The sessions hurt, and it was so painful for me to sit up to get them done. I knew I needed it, especially after learning to breathe on my own again, but, ugh, it was not fun.

I would then see the physical therapist. Her name was Michelle, and she was incredible. Our personalities meshed so well. The first day of therapy, she helped me get out of bed and introduced me to the gate belt. This was a belt that went right across my chest so it was off my incision, and she could hold on to this to catch me in case I was falling. We were going to start building up my walking strength that week. We only made it down the short hallway and back on our first try. She came by in the morning and in the afternoon every day that week. Each time she came, I was able to walk a little farther. We started off using a walker and made it around the nurses' station once and then eventually worked our way up to using no walker. The nurses would always cheer for me because they knew how big it was for me to be up and walking. I remember my body feeling so heavy, and it was so hard to keep putting one foot in front of the other. When we nearly reached my room, I began picking up speed a little. We laughed because she knew I was aware that the faster I made it back to my room, the sooner I could plop back down in my bed and take a long, deserved nap.

After physical therapy that Tuesday morning, my occupational therapist (OT) came in. She asked what I wanted to do as far as therapy, and I asked if she could help me take a shower. I had not had a shower in ten days. My hair was disgusting. It smelled and was greasy, and my body just felt gross. She agreed and was thrilled that I was up for such a challenge. I probably would not have been up for that if I knew how hard it was going to be.

Brittany, my nurse, gave us plastic coverings that would cover my incision and all my ports while I was showering. It took us a while to get all of that covered up. The shower was so small, especially with a shower chair in it. I sat in the chair to start my shower and was already exhausted by this point. My OT turned the water on and handed me the handheld hose to let the water run over my body. It felt so amazing. The warmness of the water was so comforting to me. Showers have always been my relaxing time.

My OT handed me the bar of soap, and for my therapy I had to clean myself off. She helped me with my backside and then rinsed me off. When it came to washing my hair, I could not even raise my hands up to touch it. She helped me with that and ended up washing my hair for me. I got dried off and put a new nightgown on that family and friends had brought to the hospital for me. It was nice to be out of a hospital gown. Any bit of normalcy was a comfort. I immediately lay back down, overwhelmed with exhaustion. That took all of my energy for the rest of the day. Once I was out of the shower, I realized I needed to shave my legs and armpits. One of my dear friends, Natalie Weatherford, had brought a care package to me, and it included razors, deodorant, ponytail bands, and so on. So the next time I showered, two days later, I was able to somehow muster up enough strength to shave my armpits and legs. Whew, talk about feeling like a new woman.

On the days that I did not take a shower, my OT would work with me on simple daily tasks, such as brushing my hair. Who would have thought that brushing your hair could take up all of your energy? I remember wanting to cry as I tried to brush my own hair and wanting so badly for someone to do it for me so I could crawl back in bed. One day, she had me use a balloon that a friend had brought me as a punching bag to start moving my arms. I have to admit, OT was hard and was not my favorite thing to do, but it was so essential to get me doing my normal daily routines again. Still, I dreaded every time her sweet face walked in that door.

Midday on Tuesday, we got a surprise visitor, Mark. My sister had mentioned him and asked if I remembered him. Mark had gone to the same high school we both attended but was a few years older than me. I remembered his name, and as soon as he walked into my hospital room, I immediately knew it was him. He and my sister were friends on Facebook. He had been seeing posts on Facebook about my condition and my need for a transplant.

Mark is a pilot and works for a company that flies doctors to recover organs. He had gone on a flight to recover a liver, and after his return flight home, he saw on Facebook that my sister, Laura, had posted that my liver had arrived safely and surgery should begin soon. Mark private-messaged Laura on Facebook and told her he thought he was the one who flew her sister's new liver to Dallas. Laura was shocked, and as it turns out, he was right. For him to come visit me meant so much to my family and me. Mark told us about when he got the call and how the process works. How neat that God interweaves our lives in such a way that someone I went to high school with would one day become a pilot and deliver one of the most precious gifts ever given to me.

After Mark left my hospital room, Reid and my mom and dad were the only ones left in the room. They shut the door and all gathered around my bed. I could tell by the looks on their faces, looks of sorrow, that they needed to tell me something. My dad was to my left holding my hand, Reid was to the right holding my other hand, and my mom was at the foot of my bed holding my feet.

My dad said, "Baby, we have something to tell you. We have some information on who your donor was."

I was awestruck. How had I not thought about this already or asked about this? I was quiet, and they proceeded to tell me that my donor was a fifteen-year-old female.

They said, "We wanted you to hear it from us first."

Tears filled their eyes as they started to see my reaction. I started bawling. They hugged me tight and told me that I needed to be praying for this family. They said they had begun praying for this family the day they found out about her. I was devastated that she was only fifteen. A life cut so short. I remember crying out, "Why did I live, and she died?" I had already experienced high school and college and marrying the man of my dreams. She would never get those experiences. Why her and not me? Someone had to die so I could live.

We were all crying hard by this time when a nurse came in, and my mom politely asked her to give us some time. I needed this intimate time with them to just grieve and process what had happened. I kept saying, "That is Brittany's age."

Brittany Weatherford is like a little sister to me. I grew up babysitting her. I could not imagine something happening to her at such a young age. My heart was truly aching. My family prayed with me for this family and for everything her family was facing. We prayed for a sense of comfort for her family that could only come from God alone. From then on out, my thoughts were on this family and how a precious young girl had donated her beautiful organ to save my life. I decided that day that I wanted them to know how thankful my family and I were, but more importantly that this was a gift that would be honored and treasured. I was no longer living only for myself, but also for this precious donor. I was taking care of both of us now.

Many nights, when things would calm down, Reid would sit on my bed, and we would talk. I would ask him questions about the week, and he was finally able to tell me how he was feeling. I realized that everyone was concerned about me and taking care of me, but was my family taking care of themselves? I cannot imagine how scared he and the rest of my family must have been that week. He would be talking, and I would burst into tears, and then we would both start crying, and we would just thank God for His provisions over us. Praying with your spouse is such a powerful experience.

Wednesday afternoon was, by far, the hardest day on the fourteenth floor for me. A social worker came in the late morning and was going over my recovery process with me. She was explaining what post-transplant clinic would entail. I was stunned. I had thought I would be back at work in a couple of weeks, but instead I was going to be off work at least four months, possibly six months. She began going over work with me and asking if we needed FMLA paperwork filled out. She was discussing with Reid his FMLA paperwork and what his options were for being able to stay home with me and care for me. She told me I would not be allowed to be alone for the next three months. I have always been independent and enjoyed my "me" time, and I would not have that for at least three months. She told me that after my stay on the fourteenth floor was over, I would be transferred to the Baylor Institute for Rehabilitation for at least a week, but possibly for two weeks. I was devastated that I would not be going home for some time. It was becoming more and more evident how huge an ordeal this was.

She left, and although I was shocked by the news, I was grateful we had someone to help us through this crazy and unknown process. My family stayed for a couple of hours after her visit and calmed me down by telling me how we were going to make these next few months work. I had told my mom and Reid to go home and shower and get some rest. I figured the rest of the afternoon had to be calmer than the morning was.

However, I would soon learn I was wrong about that. They left, and our dear friend Jennie, whom we travel to Ghana with, stayed with me. After my first round of occupational and physical therapy was over, I was trying to eat something small for lunch and wanted to rest before my afternoon therapy sessions started. Around lunchtime a nutritionist came in and was going to go over my new diet restrictions with me. Generally, when you are on the transplant waiting list, you have time to learn about what your new diet will be like and have time to prepare for the changes. For me this was all brand-new. She went on to tell me the things that I could never have again due to the interactions with my anti-rejection medicine. She also explained the other foods and drinks that were not good for my body anymore. I remember feeling overwhelmed while she was going over the large packet of my new diet with me. It was not that this was going to be super hard, but it was the first time I realized my life was different now. My life as I knew it was officially gone. She went into so much detail about the best choices and brands as far as milk, yogurt, and so much more. I was so glad Jennie was there to ask questions and filter some of the information for me. I was getting so overwhelmed and so tired that I was just starting to shut down. The nutritionist could tell. She had to put me on a low-potassium diet due to my numbers. She gave me meal-replacement shakes that were low in potassium to start drinking so I would be getting enough nutrients.

She began going over how to maintain health and nutrition while traveling. Without her even knowing it, she gave me the most heartbreaking news. She told me I could not travel to a third-world country safely. My heart sank to my toes. She proceeded to tell me they do not ever advise traveling to third-world countries due to the lack of clean water, food not always being thoroughly cooked, and hospitals not being developed enough for my new health needs.

I looked at Jennie with tears filling my eyes. Jennie grabbed my hand and began asking questions about this for me. My heart was shattered. Not only had my everyday normal radically changed, but I could no longer travel back to my beloved Ghana. Just the night before, I had been telling my friend Ashlee that I could not wait for her to travel to Ghana with Reid and me that summer. *What do you mean I am not going back?* Reid and I had already planned for Ghana, and I had asked for the time off work. My vacation time was supposed to be used doing mission work in Africa.

She finished going over the packet with me and told me the nutrition staff would be in and out the rest of the week to go over things with me again. The door shut behind her, and my tears were falling hard. I began bawling, and Jennie did not say a word but just held me tight. She knew there was nothing she could say to make me feel better. She knew how much Ghana meant to me and that my heart was fully invested in mission work there. God knew I needed her there in that moment to allow me to grieve.

Within several hours my world felt like it had been crushed.

Brittany, my nurse, could tell on Wednesday afternoon that I was just exhausted. I had been having too many visitors and had way too much overwhelming news given to me that day, and I was not getting the rest I needed. She put a note on my door that said for visitors to please stop by the nurses' station. Brittany would then approve who could come in and out. She even told my physical therapist that I really needed to rest and not do therapy that afternoon. I was finally able to get some rest and sleep for a few hours that afternoon. She knew exactly what I needed, and I was so thankful.

My mom and Reid got back, and they sat on my bed. I began to tell them everything that had happened while they were gone. They got tears in their eyes. They knew what I had already been through, and now, having to face this news, they could tell it was tearing me apart. That evening a group of dear friends who we call the "Ghana Girls" were coming to bring dinner and visit. We had all been traveling to Ghana together for the past five years. I told them the news, and we all started crying. We knew we would never experience Ghana together in the same way.

Wednesday was flat-out hard. Each day was quickly becoming more emotionally exhausting. When I would get overwhelmed or could feel the enemy trying to knock me down, I would just ask my family to pray over me. So many times I would call out "Jesus," whether in my head or out loud, because I knew the enemy must flee at the mention of His mighty name.

I was still not getting much sleep at night and would cry all night due to being so uncomfortable. Natalie Weatherford brought her daughter's iPad and headphones to the hospital so I could listen to music or watch movies at night when I could not sleep. The iPad also had a sound machine on it, which would drown out the loud beeps throughout the hospital halls.

Thursday was more therapy and consisted of getting up and pushing myself harder than I had been. Taking my meds was becoming harder and harder. I had never been good with taking medications. Some mornings I would take my pills and minutes later was throwing them all up. I learned that if I threw up my anti-rejection medications within an hour after taking them, I would have to retake the pills. I tried so hard to keep these down for fear of having to take them again.

Late Thursday afternoon, it was confirmed that I had been approved for physical therapy at Baylor Institute for Rehabilitation (BIR). Reid, my dad, and Jennie walked over to the therapy facility to get a tour and to see where I was going to be for the next couple of weeks. I had heard all week long about how brutal therapy at BIR can be. I knew I was in for a "boot camp" the coming week. My mom stayed with me and was such a comfort for me.

While Mom was with me, a lady came into our room and asked if I would be willing to participate in a research program. The program would ultimately not benefit me but would help people in the future having to go through a transplant. The research program was going to try to figure out early signs of rejection in patients and find common DNA factors that lead to rejection. I told her I wanted to think about it and talk to Reid first. The research was going to mean more blood draws and urine samples. After some thought I said yes to the research. I was willing to help others going through this same process in any way I could.

On Thursday one of the transplant surgeons came in for rotations and after examining my chart asked me how much I weighed. I told him what I knew I weighed before going in for surgery, and he said, "So you are thirty pounds overweight?"

I looked at him in shock. Come to find out, I had gained twenty-eight pounds of fluid from my dialysis in four days during the week of my surgeries. This was making relearning how to walk and gain my strength back even more difficult for me. He put me on a diuretic to help get some of the water weight off. My nurse, Brittany, my mom, and I still laugh about the way he asked me if I was overweight.

Friday quickly approached, and it was time to move to rehab. Friday also happened to be Valentine's Day. My mom always did special things for my sister and me for Valentine's Day. One tradition consisted of always having blueberry muffins for breakfast. Reid and my mom got me a blueberry muffin from the cafeteria that morning to keep the tradition alive even in the hospital. To my surprise I could only eat a couple of bites, as it was still so hard for me to chew and swallow.

Before moving to rehab, I was going to be able to have my ports removed, as everything from here on out would be given to me orally, and I would be stuck for blood draws daily. Brittany came in around noon to pull out my central line from my neck. She told me to take a deep breath, and when I blew out, she removed the line. It was much longer than I had anticipated. I was glad I was unconscious when these lines were put in. They had to call in another nurse to remove my dialysis port. She had to remove the sutures that were around it and then removed that port. I was so relieved to have these ports out. It burned so bad, but it felt great to have them out. I felt free. After having those removed, I had to lie down for an hour.

The staff from BIR came to get me and loaded up carts with all my flowers and essentials. I said good-bye to my sweet nurse, Brittany, and thanked her for absolutely everything. I was so grateful to have met her and for all she did for me and my family that week. Since I had to lie down for the next hour, they had to wheel me in my bed across the street. Luckily, there was an underground tunnel they were able to transport me through in my hospital bed. Each transition was a small victory but brought with it new challenges.

CHAPTER 8

OUR NEW NORMAL

Lisa

I arrived at BIR early in the afternoon. A nurse quickly came in, got us settled, and told us about what my stay would be like. It immediately had a different feel, and the room was one-third the size of my room at the hospital. Reid traded his pullout bed from our old room for a reclining chair. Even though we were not always comfortable, we found comfort just being together.

With each new move, I faced new levels of independence that I was not used to. Well, I say that, but there were definitely areas of trade-off. For example, at Baylor Hospital, Reid had been able to help me to the restroom anytime. Now, every time I needed assistance, I was to call the nurses' station and ask for help. Since they had not done an evaluation on me yet, my family was not cleared to help me out of bed. The nurses even set an alarm on my bed, so if I tried getting out, it would go off, and they would come rushing in. Being on a diuretic was not fun at all because I was having to go to the bathroom so frequently. It did not take Reid long to figure out how to turn my bed alarm off! Reid still jokes to this day about how if I give him grief, he is going to turn my bed alarm on at home.

Friday afternoon and evening, I was able to relax. My mom left for a while and picked Reid up dinner on her way back. She got him Whataburger, which is typically a staple for any Texan. I remember watching him eat and thinking that before all of this, I had taken for granted every day being able to eat normally. I so longed to do that again.

In the late evening, Reid and I were watching the Olympics, trying to keep our minds away from the unknown of the coming week. Another of those trade-offs in freedom was that the nurses' station kept getting farther away from my room with each move. This was a definite change from the days not long ago when I was watched so closely 24-7. It made us anxious because there was still that fear that something could quickly go wrong. At the same time, it was a relief that obviously the professionals knew I was improving enough to not need eyes on me at all times.

Suddenly, there was a knock on our door. It was my new respiratory therapist, Benadette. I would later refer to her as my angel, and to this day I am still convinced she is indeed an angel. Her accent immediately caught my attention. It was like an old song you have not heard in a while. The type that stirs up good feelings inside and brings back sweet memories. I asked her where she was from, and she said, "Nigeria." I felt the biggest smile come across my face.

It was as if God was calling me out and saying, "My precious daughter, you may not be able to go to Africa anymore, but I will bring Africa to you."

We told her we had traveled to Africa, and she was intrigued. We exchanged stories, and she shared with us some of the trials she had faced in her life. I shared my story from the week before with her, and she could tell I was a bit anxious about being at rehab. My doubt and fear were no match for the bold spirit living inside Benadette.

She began preaching to me and encouraging me by saying that I was in the palms of God's hands and that He would never leave me nor forsake me. That sweet, familiar accent rang out, "Honey, when you get tired, look up and call on the Mighty One. He will take care of you! When you are gaining strength to walk again, you look up. You are not taking those next steps for the doctors; you are taking them for God!"

Before she left, she shared a powerful moment of prayer with Reid and me. As the door closed behind her, I looked at Reid and, half laughing, half crying, asked, "What just happened?" It was truly another God moment. God knew exactly what I needed that night. This was a much different Valentine's Day than Reid and I were used to, but nonetheless, it was one we will cherish forever.

Saturday was my first day of therapy at BIR, and it came with a more novice schedule than during the previous week. I was very anxious about what to expect, and to be honest, getting up and moving around was the last thing I wanted to be doing.

An occupational therapist came in first and did an assessment on me. She and the physical therapist wanted to get an idea of what had happened to me and asked questions about our living conditions, such as, "Do you have stairs in your home? Do you have a walk-in shower? Do you have any pets you could possibly trip over?" And many more. I had never even thought about our home conditions. How was I ever going to get up the stairs at our apartment?

My occupational therapist for that day got me up and helped me get dressed. That was the first time in more than two weeks that I had regular clothes on. My family had to go out and buy me bigger pants since I had gained twenty-eight pounds that week. I asked them to get me the largest pants they could find because I did not want anything tight on me, especially around my incision.

It was time for my first session of physical therapy. The only problem was that I could not get my tennis shoes on. My feet were so swollen from fluid buildup and lying in bed continuously. This was no excuse for missing my first session, so with grip socks on my feet, I was ready to head to the therapy gym. Just outside my patient room was my wheelchair.

I had walked approximately fifteen feet and was already tired. After a quick wheel around the facility, it was apparent that patients with all severities of injury, disease, and circumstance were being treated at BIR. So many people were going through trials. It was tough to see.

My therapist put me on a stationary bike and had me ride for a few minutes. I had enjoyed biking before, but I was in so much pain and felt so sick. Sitting up in general hurt. Anytime I was sitting up on the bike, chair, or bed, I felt like I was being ripped in half. I knew the increased blood flow from exercise was good for my healing, but it came at a painful price.

Saturday afternoon I had an exciting surprise visitor. My transplant surgeon came to the rehab facility to check on me. I had not had a chance to meet him yet. I was amazed that he had done my transplant. I did not know how to vocalize my appreciation, but I thanked him for saving my life.

My mom was asking him questions about how I got put on the top of the list so quickly. He looked at my mom and said, "She only had about forty-eight hours to live if she did not receive a new liver."

This hit me hard. I knew I had been through a lot the week before, but I did not realize it was that bad. When you hear that you only had two days to live at most, that puts a lot of things into perspective. It was such a kind gesture for him to stop by, and I am so grateful for the post-transplant care I was given by my surgeons.

On Saturday I was progressing physically but still struggling with my appetite and eating. Nothing sounded good to me, and on top of that, swallowing was still not a normal, subconscious thing. As much trouble as I had eating, falling asleep was the hardest part at BIR for me. I would wake up constantly in pain and would just start crying.

On Sunday I had a few hours of therapy, and then I was able to get a shower Sunday night. I had an amazing night tech, Susan, who helped me shower. It was so hard to allow someone else to literally bathe every inch of me. I learned when you cannot do anything for yourself, you have to allow people to help you.

Susan was such a bright light for me that night. She told me about all of the miracles that she had seen throughout the years working at BIR. She washed my hair twice for me, and it felt so great. There is just something about someone washing your hair for you. The hot water felt so good on my tired and weak body. After my shower my relaxation was immediately dissipated through the battle of getting my pajamas on. My mom or Reid would have to blow-dry my hair, and it took everything in me to sit up for the five minutes it took to do this.

I did not sleep well again on Sunday, and Monday was a huge morning for me. I was terrified. I'd heard BIR was like boot camp, and I knew my weekend session was just a brief sample of what the coming week would be like. I received a schedule each night of what the following day would entail.

My typical day would start with a fairly early breakfast. This meal consisted of a plate of anything I could force down to go along with my side of pills. After that I would usually have a physical-therapy session followed by occupational therapy. We would mix a break time in between and do it all again in the afternoon for a total of three hours of therapy.

Monday morning I met my physical therapist that I was going to have for the rest of the week. Her name was Rachel. I just love how God knows exactly who we need in our lives at the perfect time. Rachel was a godsend. I know you have heard this numerous times. Each step of this journey welcomed a new smiling, loving face that I needed in that transitional moment. Thank You, Jesus, for this provision and grace.

Rachel and I were the same age, and our personalities clicked. Our first task was to get a baseline test of my physical levels. It was not fun. It was hard, and I must have looked at her crazy when she told me to bend down and pick up a pen off the floor. It's exactly the look you would give someone if your abdominal muscles had been cut in two not long before. Yes, that look you made right now reading this. That is the one.

Rachel was patient and encouraging with me but also pushed me because she knew what I was capable of. She wanted me to get back to as close to my old self as possible. I appreciated her methods and kindness, but after my first session, I was so anxious to crawl back into my bed. I could not wait to sleep.

No sooner than my eyes had shut, there was another knock on my door. It was my occupational therapist for the week. She was there to help me gain back my daily motor skills. She was so passionate about taking care of post-transplant patients, and it really made me feel encouraged that she was so invested. I felt like the teacher's favorite because she had such a love for transplant patients. She was so positive, and it made a difference in my dark days there.

More sleepless, tear-filled, uncomfortable nights followed. Reid, my mom, or Jennie would watch helplessly through the night as I cried myself to dozing. I cannot say I cried myself to sleep because I honestly felt I never was falling asleep. I plugged in my headphones and turned on the sound machine to drown out the beeps I could hear in other rooms around me.

My night nurse on Wednesday gave me a muscle relaxer, and for the first time, I finally slept five hours straight. But like clockwork, they came to start drawing my blood, and it was time to wake up for breakfast and pills.

Therapy was brutal. At times, the days seemed to fly by. My days were consumed with a strict schedule of therapy, attempting to eat meals, taking my medications, and meeting with doctors and nutritionists. My family and friends would come by throughout the day and come to therapy with me. They enjoyed seeing the progress I was making. I was proud of myself, too. One exercise at a time, my strength was coming back.

On Thursday, I had progressed so much that I thought for sure I was going to be released that weekend. I did not want to spend another long weekend at BIR. Unfortunately, my therapist and doctor met and decided that I was not quite ready to be released. I cried when they told me this. I was so ready to be home.

They decided to give me a pass so I could leave for the day, but I had to come back that night. I could leave and go eat somewhere or even go home for a few hours if I wanted. The thought of going out to eat at a restaurant and sitting up for a long period of time sounded awful to me. We decided to make the best of it and make our first trip back home.

On Saturday morning, February 22, after I took my meds and let them settle for a couple of hours, we made the trek home. Being in the car for the first time was physically uncomfortable and weird. Each bump felt like it jostled my abdomen.

It was also very emotional for me. I remember staring at people in their cars and thinking, *How are they all so happy right now? It must be nice to be able to drink that thirty-two-ounce Coke or run to catch the DART train.* I could not believe that I had been "locked up" in the hospital for so long and so many millions of people were just living their lives outside the hospital walls.

We drove to Paradise Bakery Café, and Reid went inside to get us our favorite salad as my treat for getting to go home. He went inside, and I started bawling in the car. I remember yelling out, "Thank You, Jesus. Thank You." I could not say it enough. I just had to cry out to God and thank Him for saving my life. When we pulled up at the apartment, I started crying again and just kept thinking, *I have had a liver transplant.* It had been two weeks since my transplant, but I was still in shock.

Opening the door into our home felt so weird. It took me a few minutes to get up the seventeen stairs to our apartment. When I arrived home, I immediately saw the note on the fridge that Reid had left me a couple of weeks before: "Welcome home, Mrs. Barker." Tears filled my eyes, and I praised God that I was finally home to read that note at last.

During our field trip home, as we called it, we had to do home assessments. This included making sure I could get in and out of the bathtub with Reid's assistance. I checked to see if I could sit on the toilet and walk up and down the stairs. Getting up and down the stairs was one of the biggest concerns for my doctors and therapist and something I had to be cleared on before going home permanently.

Rachel had me practice on the stairs so much at BIR. I hated it, but I knew it was essential for my everyday life. It was like preparing for a driving test or a marathon. Maybe both. We had to rearrange furniture around our apartment so that I would be able to sit and rest while walking to and from rooms if I needed it. Reid did some laundry while I lay in our own bed, and before we knew it, it was time to head back to BIR. I was devastated when we had to go back. I just wanted to stay in the comfort of my own quiet home.

On Sunday, I had a rough day. I had no therapy, which gave me way too much time with my thoughts. My back was starting to hurt from lying down all the time. I was sore and restless. I had the opportunity to leave the building and go on another "field trip" if I wanted to, but I could not muster up enough strength. Instead, I had my mom and Reid wheel me outside in my wheelchair. We sat outside, and my mom just rubbed my back as tears streamed down my face. I remember Reid looking at me, and there was nothing anyone could say to make me feel better. Although I was taking baby steps in my physical recovery, the whole process was becoming so overwhelming. I was anxious to get out of rehab, but at the same time, I knew the recovery and battle ahead of me at home. Going home meant that the life I'd known was never going to be the same.

Monday, February 24, was my last full day of rehab and Reid's birthday. I have always loved birthdays. I love celebrating my own birthday, celebrating other people's birthdays, and making people feel important and loved on their special day. I felt helpless that year, not being able to get Reid a birthday card or a gift or to spoil him for all he had done for me, especially the past three weeks. My family finally convinced me to allow them to buy a card for Reid from me. It took me probably thirty minutes to write in the card because I was so weak.

My occupational therapist was so awesome that Monday. She let me bake Reid brownies for my therapy that day in the rehab center's kitchen. It helped me use my wrists and practice getting back into the routine in the kitchen. She provided all the groceries for me, and it was truly so thoughtful. We somehow made Reid stay in my room and brought him down when the brownies were finished. It was such a special moment for me. I was so proud to be able to do something so simple for my precious husband.

My therapy concluded that Monday afternoon, and it was bittersweet for me to say good-bye to all of my therapists. They brought me so far in my recovery while I was at BIR, and I am forever grateful for them.

Late Monday afternoon, a lady from the transplant team at the hospital came to BIR to go over my transplant binder with me. This binder was my guide to going home as a transplant recipient. She went over each of my medications with me in detail. All fifteen of them. I started out listening intently but began fading toward the end.

I was so overwhelmed. I went from taking only birth control once a day to having to take fifteen meds two times a day. There was so much information she had to review: identifying what the pills looked like, following the binder's instructions on when to take them and not following what the bottle said, taking my temperature two times a day, and watching for signs of infection and rejection, just to name a few.

It was just another reminder of how different life was now going to look. All I could think about was, *How are we ever going to be able to work all of this into our old normal routine?* I was exhausted emotionally and physically, and I took a long nap after that meeting.

On Monday night, our families got together to celebrate Reid. We ordered pizza, and his mom decorated the tables in the lobby. I was so thankful he was able to feel special and adored that night. I love this quote from Martin Luther King Jr.: "The ultimate measure of a man is not where he stands in moments of comfort and convenience, but where he stands at times of challenge and controversy." Reid never wavered from his faith and stood strong during every challenge for the entire month of February.

I was able to make it down to eat one slice of pizza slowly, and then I started hurting. It still hurt so bad to sit up in a chair. I started crying, and Reid, of course, even on his special day, was the first one to comfort me. My family gathered around me and began to pray. I went upstairs, and Reid helped me make it to the restroom. When I came out, Reid was lying in my rehab bed. He said, "It's my birthday. I get the bed; you're in the pullout chair." Of course, he was just kidding, and it made me laugh so much. He is always making me smile, and I so needed it that night.

Tuesday, February 25, rolled around quickly, and it was my day to officially go home. I had been admitted to the hospital on February 2. I was so ready to be home, but the thought of going home was terrifying. Not being under the constant care of my doctors and nurses was so scary. Reid never told me, but I can imagine it was nerve-racking for him as well, being the main one taking care of me at home. The pharmacist came into my room and delivered all of my medications. I was having a rough morning and could not keep my medicine down. We waited a couple of hours until my stomach settled down, and I was able to ride in the car. We said our good-byes to the staff at BIR, and that was emotional. I am forever grateful for all of my nurses, techs, doctors, and surgeons, and all the staff at Baylor Plano, Baylor Dallas, and BIR. We still try to stop by and visit them when we can and remind them of how grateful we are for the role they all played in saving my life.

Ms. Ruthie, one of my dearest techs whom I grew to love at BIR, walked me out to the car. She gave me a huge hug and wished us the best of luck. And just like that, Reid and I were headed home.

It was so emotional being home. It was a huge miracle that I had walked through those doors again, and Reid and I were very aware of that. It was very strange being home at the same time. Strange to not hear the beeping sounds from the hospital halls and have a nurse coming in every so often to check on me. It was strange not getting woken up to take meds.

I had high expectations for my first night's rest at home. I had been eagerly awaiting sleep in my own bed for weeks now, and it turned out to be a disappointment. Surprisingly, the hospital bed was nice for lifting my upper body up because I was experiencing trouble breathing. No matter the amount of pillows I put underneath me, it was just not comfortable. Our bed was lower than the hospital bed and was just all-around hard. I was having to get up every couple of hours to use the bathroom, as I was still on a diuretic. Reid was so gentle and so precious with me and did not make a fuss even once about waking up multiple times a night to take care of my every need, including lifting me out of the bed.

The first morning home, we had an appointment scheduled to meet my outpatient physical therapist at Baylor Plano. To be honest, I was dreading setting foot back in that place. It was an eerie feeling for me. It was the place where it all started, and my last memories at that place were making me feel miserable.

I was going to have a male therapist for the first time since I'd started this journey, and I was unsure about that. Once again, God provided another perfect person for Reid and me on this journey. God gave us Hunter. Hunter was more than we could have hoped for in my outpatient physical therapist. He was close in age to us and understood how our life had just gotten turned upside down. Only God could orchestrate the fact that Reid's older sister and Hunter were in Sunday school class together years ago and that Hunter's grandmother and Reid's nana were friends. This strengthened our bond with Hunter immediately.

He was very knowledgeable in post-transplant care and specialized in abdomen work. He immediately helped break up scar tissue near my incision and told Reid and me what we needed to be doing at home. He taught me how to get my breathing back on track and how to relax and focus on deep breaths. Therapy was simple at first, but as I got stronger, the workouts got harder. The first time I saw Hunter, he did a set of tests on me, and I was so weak. My results for these tests blew my mind. I knew I would be slow and weak, but I was shocked at how slow and weak I was. During my three months with Hunter, he helped me gain my strength and energy back, and by the time I left him, I was walking a mile on the treadmill, doing squats and lunges, and breathing normally.

The first three months at home were tough. We had to attend liver clinic two times a week, on Mondays and Thursdays, for three months post-transplant. This consisted of arriving at the hospital at six thirty in the morning; getting my blood drawn; eating breakfast (which was still a major challenge); taking thirty minutes to get my dreaded medicine down; and attending six weeks of classes on caring for my new liver, recognizing signs of infection and rejection, and nutrition. Then we would wait to see the nurses and, eventually, the transplant surgeons. They would go over the lab work from earlier that morning and would make any changes necessary to my medications and course of treatment. Some days I would leave with encouraging reports, and other days I felt like we were backtracking. Nonetheless, we had a huge support system that was waiting with open arms to serve us and lift up our prayer requests to a mighty God. Thursdays at clinic were lab work only, at six thirty in the morning. The rest of our days were filled with hematology appointments and therapy. It felt like a full-time job.

Reid was able to be home with me until after spring break. He went back to work on Tuesday, March 18, 2014. I was devastated when he had to leave me. I understood that he needed to and that I was stable enough, but we had just spent the past month and a half living both our darkest moments and our sweetest, most tender moments that we had experienced in our marriage thus far. It was hard for him to go back to work as well. Then, I had what I called the "babysitters club." This consisted of our closest family and friends who rotated days and took care of my every need while Reid was at work, including preparing meals for me, helping me in and out of bed, taking me to therapy, washing dishes and clothes, praying and encouraging me, and being a shoulder for me to cry on when I was having a dark day. These people were precious to us during this time.

Reid still took every Monday off until I was released from transplant clinic. Those Mondays were priceless days that I am grateful I had with him by my side. Even with the babysitters club, I would still want Reid to come home from work as soon as he could. I missed him and felt the most comfortable when he was caring for me. He would work all day and then come home and take care of my every need. I would always wait to shower until he got home. He had to help me in and out of the shower. I had a shower chair. He would have to start the water for me and hand me the handheld shower handle, and I would rinse myself off. He would be near so that when I hollered that I was done, he could help me out of the shower carefully. I was still at high risk for clotting and could not risk falling during this time. Taking a shower would wipe me out. I had never imagined being so aware of what a blessing it was to shower on my own.

Taking my pills was a constant battle for me. Reid was the sweetest and would turn on Christian music and sit in the kitchen with me for an hour until I got all my medications down. Then he would help me sit still for an hour so none of them came back up. He was patient with me while we discovered that drinking Powerade was going to be the best way to get my medication down. He never once got frustrated and just kept telling me that we could do this. It was a new normal, but we were going to be able to figure it all out. He ended up being right, but at the time, I was overwhelmed with my days consisting of doctors' visits, pills, blood work, therapy, and resting.

I remember the first night I called my mom from Reid's phone. I did not turn my phone on for about a month after my transplant. I was too overwhelmed to look at people's sweet messages and concerns for me, and I was having trouble with my vision due to the high doses of steroids. When my mom answered the phone, she thought it was Reid. When I said, "Hi, Mommy," she just burst into tears. Reid would always joke with me about how much I call my mom. Our nightly ritual after work was to always call each other on the ride home. We obviously had not gotten to do that in a little over a month.

She was just bawling and then stopped and said, "There was a time when I did not know if I would ever hear your voice on the phone again."

This choked me up. I was realizing more and more what my family had gone through during that week of transplant, how scared they must have been, and how they had not known if they would ever get their loved one back the way she was prior to transplant.

My recovery time at home was also spent with many sweet family members and friends feeding us dinner nightly. It was such a blessing to not have to worry about meals. I had many restrictions during this time, and our dear friend Lacy was an angel setting everything up for us.

After dinner, Reid or my mom would take me for a walk. The weather was starting to turn nice, and the fresh air felt good. We would make it across the street to a park, and I would be exhausted. I would sit on the edge of the slide and rest for a while before mustering up enough strength to walk home.

I graduated from liver clinic on April 28, 2014. This was such a glorious day for us. This meant that I was released to the care of my family physician and would not be seeing the transplant team until my one-year biopsy unless something went wrong. I began to go to my family physician once a week for a month for labs, and then every other week for a month, and then once a month.

I will continue with this monthly lab draw for two years post-transplant, and then it will go to every three months for the rest of my life. My lab reports are read by my family physician and are sent to my transplant team for them to review. If anything looks suspicious, they contact me to make changes in my meds or request more testing. After being watched like a hawk for so many months, it is scary moving on with life and being released from the transplant team's care.

When I was released, we were assigned a transplant coordinator who helped us with anything and everything we needed. Reid and I felt safe knowing that Angie, whom we have grown to love, was always just a call or an e-mail away.

I gained enough strength to go back to work in June. However, this proved to be too soon. I was still much weaker than I thought. I continued with my physical-therapy exercises for another month before attempting to work again. As great as

I felt daily not working, getting back into work was a whole new ball game. In July, I started back just two mornings a week for a couple of hours at a time. That turned into two half days, and, finally, on October 1, 2014, I worked my first full day. I would soon work two full days a week for the rest of 2014. Starting January 2015, I was back three full days a week, and starting the first week of March 2015, I was back three and a half days a week.

I am still taking anti-rejection medications every twelve hours, which I will do the rest of my life. This prevents my body from trying to reject my new organ. I give blood for lab work one to two times a month and take chemotherapy orally five nights a week. I still have my blood disease, and the chemotherapy helps suppress my platelets so my blood does not become too thick and clot again. I have follow-up visits with my specialist regularly, and they are on top of monitoring my levels and making sure everything is stable. I thank God for giving my doctors the wisdom to treat me.

It is very nice to have a routine back in our lives. I never thought we would manage to fit our new normal into our old normal, but we did. The process has been long and hard but worth it nonetheless. To look back and see how far we have come since the day we arrived home from the hospital is truly incredible. It has been nothing short of constant miracles and provisions from God.

Physical therapist, Rachel

Welcome home gift from Natalie and Jennie containing comments from my Caring Bridge site and bible verses to comfort me during recovery

Reid's sister and her family Barrett, Katie, and Lennox

Transplant nurse, Brittany

Outpatient physical therapist, Hunter

Transplant nurse, Lauren

CHAPTER 9

WHY NOT ME?

Lisa

"Why you?" This was a question I heard over and over during my recovery process. And to be completely honest, it was a question I would end up hating. This question bothered me from the beginning. People's intent was so genuine when they would ask me, "How could something so awful happen to someone like you who is so close to the Lord?" They were being compassionate, but it irked me.

The question I started asking them back from day one was, "Why not me?" None of us are entitled to good health. Christ promised us that we would face pain and trials on this earth and said to be prepared because they are coming. But He also promised us that He has overcome the world, and one day I will be safe in His arms and will not feel this pain any longer. Any suffering now is not worth comparing to the eternal glory that is coming.

The point of our journey was never about us. It was about something so much greater. I never had pity for myself. The point was never my pain or how my life would now be different. I was freed because I was not the point. God took complete control of my story, my pain, and my new lifestyle. He was the point from the very beginning. This journey was and is all for His sake. He worked the miracle in my life and has been the main character of my story since day one and will continue to be. All glory goes to Him.

I kept picturing Christ dying on the cross every time I heard this question. The pain that Christ endured on that cross was more pain than you or I could ever imagine enduring. Because of that suffering He went through, I have an eternal future to look forward to where I will no longer have a blood disease or have to worry about taking anti-rejection medicine and being on chemotherapy. I will be healthy, whole, and complete again in the arms of my Savior.

However, with that being said, I also would find myself thinking, *Why did God choose me to live? Why am I a survivor?* I still had so many blessings even in the midst of tragedy.

I am definitely not the same person I was before this journey. I have learned to be truly grateful for every single day. I have learned to enjoy each day and count my blessings and provisions that surround me on a daily basis. The fact that we wake up each morning and are healthy enough to get out of bed, go to work, and speak with our family and friends is such a special gift given to us by the Lord. I have learned that every day is an opportunity to be a blessing to someone else. When I first got out of the hospital and would go out in public to go to outpatient physical therapy, I remember thinking, *So many people are walking past me and have no idea about the battle I am facing.* I soon found an anonymous quote that will resonate with me always: "Everyone you meet is fighting a battle you know nothing about. Be kind. Always." Every single person we come into contact with is going through something in life. Your kind gestures can always be the difference in someone's day.

Our family and friends taught us how to love others well. They showed us how to be bold in caring for those in need. They taught us about praying with families in need and about how the best thing you can do for those in the hospital is to drop by with food or a care package, give your love, and let the family know they are in your thoughts and prayers. Those were my favorite visitors. Staying in the hospital for an extended amount of time can be difficult and exhausting. But knowing that people dropped by to see us and gave their love meant the world to us. I have deeply learned more about being the Body of Christ, and I am forever grateful for that.

I believe there is pure joy in our sufferings. I also believe that God finds joy in the way we handle our sufferings. We should carry hope in our sufferings so that a watching world may see that Jesus is enough. My prayer through this journey has been that people would see that God is enough. I never questioned why this journey happened to me. Instead, I felt honored that God handpicked me for this journey. What an honor. It has been a hard journey and one that Reid and I never would have chosen for ourselves, but we are so grateful God chose it for us.

I know that God worked a miracle in my life that snowy February day in 2014. He chose for me to still live on this earth. I don't believe that being here on earth beats the alternative. That alternative is being at the feet of Jesus. However, I am blessed for the time still here on earth with my family and loved ones, and I know that my purpose on earth is to glorify and honor God for who He is and all that He has done in my life. He has given me this story as my testimony, and it is to be shared to further His kingdom.

God is good. He is faithful. He is never changing. He is constant. He is the master physician, and He is worthy of all praises. My prayer will continue to be that through our journey, people will see all these characteristics of God and will run into His open and loving arms and that they will find comfort in my favorite verse, Psalms 46:10: "Be still, and know that I am God." When life is hectic and spinning out of your control, may you be still and remember that He is God. He is to be exalted in all the nations and on earth, He has you in the palm of His hand, and He is in control.

"Sometimes life takes us places we never expected to go. And in those places God writes a story we never thought would be ours" (Renee Swope).

God, Your ways are higher than ours, and Your thoughts are higher and better than ours. Thank You for choosing us for this journey. It is an honor to serve You and live out the testimony You continue to provide for us. All glory goes to You forever and ever.

Reid

One of my favorite sermons from our pastor, Matt Chandler, was from Jesus's Sermon on the Mount in Matthew 7:24–27. In this passage Jesus describes two different types of people. Those who truly listen to Jesus's words and do them are wise and build their house or life on the foundation of Christ. Those who do not listen and do not heed the words of God build their house and foundation on sand, and the storms sweep it away. As many times as I had heard this message and read it growing up, it wasn't until I heard Matt preach this particular sermon that the truths of those verses really stood out to me. You see, even though the wise person had built his or her house on the rock, it did not prevent the storms from coming. Both houses faced the same elements. The one that had its foundation planted firmly in the truths of Christ was able to withstand the storm.

That story is a representation of our lives. We need that firm foundation of a life built around faith in our relationship with our Savior. That foundation does not keep the storms of life from hitting us and testing our support. Yet it does ensure that after the floodwaters disappear and the clouds dissipate, our relationship and hope in Christ will still be standing strong.

So why not us? It is a question that seems to get answered every day for Lisa and me. Maybe God chose us because we are young! So many people have been blown away by the fact that these health issues and emergencies took place so early in our life and marriage. What a blessing that God gave this to us at twenty-five years old so we can have much more life and energy to tell His story. We have been given the gift of time to use His miracle to praise His name.

Maybe God chose us so that we could better encourage others going through similar troubles. The Bible says in 2 Corinthians 1:3–4, "Blessed be the God and Father of our Lord Jesus Christ, the Father of mercies and God of all comfort, who comforts us in all our affliction, so that we may be able to comfort those who are in any affliction, with the comfort with which we ourselves are comforted by God."

Maybe God chose us because a young girl needs encouragement that taking pills for the rest of her life to keep her alive can serve as a daily reminder to honor her donor and God with her life—so she can see she can be confident in the transplant scars she carries. They are beautiful scars that tell a bigger story. It is a life-giving story that is to be celebrated. Maybe God chose us so that I could be an encourager to a husband who is forced by unexpected circumstances to become a caretaker—a young man who does not expect his young bride to be nearly taken from him and needs that reassurance that God has equipped him to stand by her side and get through this storm together.

Maybe God chose us because He knew you would pick up this book right now. Maybe we went through this trial in our lives so God could have you in this exact spot to fully reveal His love and calling in your life. Maybe God chose us because that is how He chose you! Do not leave anything undone. The beauty of all of this is there is nothing that you have to do other than to acknowledge His love for you. He died on the cross for your sins and rose in three days, defeating death, so you could have an eternal life of salvation in Him. It is grace through faith, not by works. That is the peace we have had through all this. To live is Christ, but to die is gain. If death is the worst thing that can happen, then I will count it as joy to be with my loving Savior. Maybe God chose us because if you just gave your life to Christ, it is all worth it. In delivering us, maybe He delivered you.

CHAPTER 10

THE GIFT OF LIFE

Lisa

I have said it a million times since my transplant, and I will continue to say it: organ donation is the absolute most treasured gift you can give to another human. When I woke up from surgery and learned about my donor, Courtney, I immediately knew that I was no longer living for myself.

I have come to realize that God's plan is perfect even if we do not always understand it. He took Courtney's life on earth on February 4, 2014, but I cannot help but realize how He is still using her. He is still using her cherished life to impact others. So many organ donors have been registered because of hearing of the gift of life that Courtney gave me and four other individuals. This was God's purpose for Courtney's life—to impact so many lives on earth and then to continue to impact lives and further His kingdom even when she was taken away from us.

Because of this plan, I will live each day to glorify and honor God first and foremost, and recognize that I am no longer living for just God and myself but also for Courtney Ray Sterling. She left an amazing legacy, and my job is to continue her legacy. She gave the ultimate gift so others may live. Her gift has affected not only the recipients but their families and friends. She did not just save one person; she saved families and communities from complete heartbreak.

I am blessed beyond words with a second chance at life. I wake up and go to bed grateful. Grateful that I still have time with my family and friends and can still make an impact on this world. I was beyond devastated when I found out in the hospital that it would not be a good idea to travel back to Ghana, Africa. I was not sure what my mission or purpose would be now. God is so sweet to His children. I never should have doubted that God's plan for the next step of my life would be more beautiful than I could have dreamed up myself.

I have become a passionate advocate for raising awareness about the importance of organ donation. Every chance I get to share my story and tell someone that I would not be standing in front of him or her if it was not for the gift of organ donation moves me beyond measure. To see people's faces as they realize the ultimate gift is incredible.

The beauty of organ donation is how closely it reflects Christ's love for us through the Gospel—selflessly giving life to someone else who cannot repay that gift just as Jesus did for us. As humans we are all sinners in need of grace and a sacrifice. Through Jesus's death we were given that chance for a transplant. In His death our diseased heart is washed clean by the blood of Christ. We are given that second opportunity for life. That is organ donation. That is the Gospel. It is so comforting to know that Courtney knew Christ as her Lord and Savior. We can rest in the fact that we will see her again.

The time spent here completing our journey will seem short in comparison to the endless amount of time that we will share with our Savior and loved ones someday. We find hope in that fact, and we praise God that truly to live is Christ and to die is gain. It is now our purpose to use the rest of our time honoring Courtney by glorifying our God.

The reality is that the lives that Courtney has impacted are endless. We will never know this side of heaven how many lives she has touched. I refer to it as a ripple effect. Because of my life being saved, so many of our family and friends have registered as organ donors. We never know when we will be called home or the lives that could potentially be saved from Courtney saving my life. It goes on and on.

Thanks to the gift we were given through organ donation, we have had the most incredible opportunity to meet our donor family. From the first day my family told me about Courtney, I knew that I wanted to meet this family. I quickly realized that they may never want to meet me, but I knew I at least wanted to send them a letter to thank them for the gift they had given to me and my family.

I used to say that being an organ donor was a simple decision. I had only thought of that decision being made while at the DPS renewing my driver's license. But when a family is approached about their loved one being a candidate for organ donation, it is no longer a simple decision. It is a very selfless decision. That family is in the midst of their darkest days, and for them to see past their pain and hurt and to think of other families who are on the verge of losing their loved ones, if the gift of an organ is not given to them, is truly remarkable and so selfless.

That family for me was the Sterling family.

I decided to write my letter of thanks to them on July 26, 2014. This was just shy of six months after the transplant and the loss of their beautiful daughter. I sat down to write this letter and started bawling. I sat there asking God, "How do I find the words to thank this family for the gift of life?"

God definitely stopped me in my tracks, and I could clearly hear Him saying, "You should be utterly speechless every morning you wake up and I have given you another day of life."

I immediately picked up my pen and began to write. God was so clear. He spoke truth into me—because of this family's gift and His gift, I am alive today. I am alive to make a difference in this world and share the testimony that He has given me.

I began to express my gratitude to the Sterlings for the gift they had given me. I was able to tell them I had celebrated my twenty-sixth birthday and our two-year wedding anniversary because of the special gift I was given. I told them that Reid and I and our families and friends have been praying for them daily, and the prayers will continue always. I expressed that I would love to hear back from them and keep in contact. I prayed fervently over that letter in the post-office parking lot for fifteen minutes, asking that God would prepare my donor parents' hearts for the letter that would soon be arriving in their mailbox. A letter that would most likely catch them off guard. A letter that had the potential to change their lives forever. I finally gathered the courage to place it in the blue box and drove away with tears flowing down my face.

I had prepared my heart that I might never hear back from them. And to be honest, I had come to peace with that as long as they knew how grateful I was for them and their decision to donate their daughter's organs.

Two months went by, and I had not heard anything. I continued to pray fervently for this family daily. On October 1, 2014, which happened to be my first full day back at work, I came home and checked the mail. When I saw the return address, my heart started racing. It was a letter from the Southwest Transplant Alliance, and I knew in my gut it was the return letter from the Sterlings.

I ran inside and was screaming for Reid. I said several times over, "This is it. This is it."

I quickly opened it, and three pictures of Courtney fell out of the envelope. I grabbed them and started crying. We walked to the couch and looked at the pictures and kept saying how beautiful she was.

I found out that night that my organ donor was Courtney Ray Sterling. She was beautiful and had a smile that was contagious. The letter was written by my donor mom, Dawn Sterling. I started reading the letter out loud to Reid, and we both just stopped after the first two sentences and started bawling. I cannot remember another time that I cried so hard. Once we gathered ourselves to finish the letter, it was evident how amazing and strong this family was.

The letter gave me insight into Courtney and who she was, and Dawn told me she wanted to tell me anything and everything that I wanted to know about Courtney. She wrote that she would love to meet and keep in contact if we desired to do so. On the back page, she wrote in big letters, "P.S. Happy Belated Birthday and Anniversary." I started bawling once again. The thought that a mother who will never get to say those words to her daughter again so joyfully said them to me struck me to the core. I looked at Reid and said, "She is amazing."

I immediately called my mom and told her she had to come over quickly. I learned in that moment that you never call family frantically after you have had a transplant because they automatically think something is wrong. I assured her I was physically fine but that I had heard from my donor family. I let the rest of my family know, and we all cried and thanked God for answered prayers.

That night we gained additional family members in the Sterlings.

The next day, I filled out the form to release my information to the Sterlings. As long as they signed the release form as well, we would soon have each other's phone numbers and other personal information released from the amazing staff at the Southwest Transplant Alliance. The Southwest Transplant Alliance is the organ procurement organization (OPO) who coordinated my transplant. I cannot say enough good things about the staff at the Southwest Transplant Alliance and the lifesaving work they do. They work around the clock advocating for all recipients.

On October 16, 2014, I received their information. I was full of anticipation and nervousness at the same time. I waited to call the Sterlings until Friday, October 17. Reid had the idea to text message Dawn first so that we did not catch her completely off guard. I was anticipating not hearing back from her for a while, but she texted me back a couple of minutes later, and we set up a phone call for a few minutes after that.

My heart was beating so fast as I dialed her number. When Dawn answered, my stomach was in a knot. She immediately put me on speaker so that Michael, her husband, could hear our conversation as well. I thanked them immediately for the gift of life. They said there was no need to thank them, and they were so glad that I was doing well. They told me about Courtney, Connely, and Tyson and how they had lost both of their beautiful daughters and their unborn grandson in a car accident. I told them about my health issues and what had led me to needing Courtney's precious liver.

I had a question that had been on my mind since after I received Courtney's liver. I said, "I know this might sound strange, but I have to ask you if Courtney liked Cheetos."

They said she loved Cheetos and was always sneaking them into the cart when they would go to the store. I told them that when I got home from the hospital, the nutritionists were telling me to eat anything I wanted or could to gain weight at the time. I told my family that I wanted the biggest bag of Cheetos that they could find, and they looked at me with the strangest look on their faces. I liked Cheetos, but I had not had them since high school and never would have bought them at the store. I was craving them so much, and I ate the entire bag of Cheetos by myself. It was a connection to Courtney, and it was special for me.

I was able to share with them that I had gotten very involved with volunteering with the Southwest Transplant Alliance and had a speaking engagement coming up. Dawn said she wanted to come and would be there to support me. We visited on the phone for forty-five minutes, and I was just in awe when we got off the phone. They are the most incredible people, and I am so very grateful that they have opened their hearts and lives to us.

I sent them pictures of Reid and me and my family right away so they could see what I looked like. We texted back and forth, and two weeks later Dawn flew to Dallas so we could meet.

The morning she came to meet us, November 2, 2014, I was a nervous wreck. I was very emotional, and Reid and I sat in our living room and prayed and prayed before she arrived.

Hugging Dawn for the first time was a moment I will never forget. Reid happened to capture our first hug on camera. I was filled with joy that Dawn was getting to hold part of her baby again. We spent all day together getting to know each other and learning more about her family. She met my entire family that day and was such a trouper. She came with me to my speaking engagement, and the relationship we have built since that weekend has been astounding.

Dawn has come into town every month since. I was able to meet Michael on February 6, 2015, exactly one year to the date that his daughter saved my life. My family had a one-year celebration of life and honoring of Courtney that weekend, and Dawn and Michael were there to be with us. In May 2015, Reid and I were able to travel to Beaumont for the first time to visit Michael and Dawn and to see where Courtney was from. It was beyond special for me to be able to see where Courtney lived, see where she went to school, meet more of her extended family, watch her color-guard team perform, meet her friends, and see her beautiful grave site. It was a very emotional and incredible weekend. Reid and I grew even closer with Michael and Dawn.

Dawn and Michael started calling the recipients their "God children," and I absolutely love it.

We traveled back to Beaumont in October 2015 to spend the weekend at the Sterlings' beach cabin, and it was such a relaxing time with them, a time when we did not have anywhere to be and could just fully enjoy one another's company. We laughed and made jokes and officially have so many inside jokes that only we would understand. We hate telling them good-bye at the airport and miss them terribly when we are not with them. It keeps us all going to start planning our next visit as soon as we leave.

We have all been blessed with the extreme honor of being participants in the 2016 Tournament of Roses Parade in Pasadena, California, on New Year's Day. I was asked to represent the Southwest Transplant Alliance as a float rider, and Courtney was honored as a donor and had her own floragraph on the Donate Life Rose Parade float. There were twenty-four float riders who were all recipients, sixty floragraphs representing sixty heroes who gave the gift of life, and twelve walkers who were all living donors. Reid and I traveled with Michael and Dawn to

Pasadena, California, for six days. Our time was filled with lots of events honoring organ donation and the gift of life given by donor families from across the United States. It was an incredibly special time for us to meet other donor and recipient families. There is something very powerful about being around others who understand 100 percent the struggle you have walked. It was emotional but an exciting time for us, and we feel so incredibly blessed that we had the honor to share our story of hope through organ donation with the world. We made memories and friends on this trip that will last a lifetime. One thing that was evident during this trip was that no one asked to be in the situations they were in. No donor family ever wanted to lose a loved one, and no recipient ever wished to be on the transplant list and need a new organ. However, it is what you do with the situation you are given that matters. Reid and I, along with the Sterlings, have decided to share our story to inspire others that there is a silver lining to each circumstance. I truly cannot imagine not having the Sterlings in my life. I am grateful that God handpicked this incredible family to be my angels.

It has been our complete joy to learn more about Courtney and Connely. They were both absolutely beautiful. They were not concerned with popularity or the way others looked. They loved and welcomed everyone into their lives. Connely and Dawn could pass for twins. Connely was looking forward to being a mom to baby Tyson. She had a heart of gold and loved people well.

Courtney was very involved in band and color guard. She was a social butterfly. She had so many friends, made everyone laugh, always had a joke for her friends, and gave them each a special emoji icon on her iPhone.

These girls were loved fiercely by their parents. They were always 100 percent provided for and had love surrounding them at all times. Their lives were cut drastically short, but their time spent here on earth made a difference in the lives of others. They left behind a lifetime of memories and special legacies.

Dawn and Michael are indeed my "God parents." They have taken Reid and me in and have loved us like their own. They are so strong. They both have hearts of gold. They go out of their way to make others feel loved and comfortable around them. They are our new extended family.

They now are walking through life with us and share in our milestones. They are supportive and so encouraging of our dreams and aspirations, which are made possible because of the gift of life given to me from their precious daughter Courtney.

Courtney, I anxiously await the day I get to wrap my arms around you in heaven and personally thank you for the gift you have given me. Until then, I will continue to let everyone know that the greatest hero I never knew was my organ donor, Courtney, who saved my life.

Meeting my Godmother, Dawn for the first time

Amber Rhoades (Courtney's Aunt), Lisa, and Dawn with matching Michael Kors' purses, The green represents organ donation

Raising organ donor awareness at the Tim McGraw concert in Dallas

Photo session with photographer and friend, Natalie Christine Photography

One year celebration and honoring of Courtney's life

Michael, Dawn, Lisa, Reid, Yvonne, Harold
(Courtney's Grandparents)

Reid's Family

Lisa's Family

Rose Parade 2016

Photo Credit: Scott Weersing

Photo Credit: Scott Weersing

Courtney Ray Sterling School Photo 2014

Courtney Color Guard 2014

The Sterling Family: Connely, Dawn, Michael, Courtney

Unfortunately, not all stories end like ours. Due to a shortage of registered organ donors, people die every day on the transplant waiting list. Myths surrounding organ donation are very common reasons why people do not choose to sign up. I encourage you to do your own research on the beauty of organ donation. Our hope is that through sharing our story, you have seen the beauty that organ donation can bring out of tragedy. It is now our life mission to help others who are in need experience that beauty.

According to organdonor.gov, in 2015 there were more than 121,552 individuals in the United States alone waiting for the gift of a lifesaving transplant and a second chance at life. Every ten minutes, a new name is added to the national transplant waiting list.

More than thirteen thousand people in our home state of Texas are waiting for a lifesaving transplant.

More than eight million Texans have already registered their decision to donate and save lives.

A single organ and tissue donor can save or improve the lives of up to fifty different people.

By the end of the day today, seventy-one people will receive the organ transplant they need to survive. Twenty-two people will die today because that gift was not available.

We know it is a hard truth to face that someday we will not be here. Still, how special to think that you could continue to live on through giving life to someone else. Would you consider being an organ, eye, and tissue donor? Our dream is to see that number of twenty-two people dying daily from not receiving an organ decrease each and every year. We are grateful that our hero helped that happen. God bless you all.

—Team Barker

Please visit donatelifetexas.org if you reside in Texas or donate life.net for all other states to find more information on organ, eye, and tissue donation and register your decision to save lives today.

Website: teambarkerdelivered.com
Facebook: Team Barker Delivered
Instagram: @teambarkerdelivered
Twitter: @TeamBarker12

Made in the USA
Middletown, DE
25 May 2016